the *gluten-free*
INSTANT POT®
COOKBOOK

The Gluten-Free Instant Pot Cookbook is packed with time-saving tips, insights on creating flavors reflective of various ethnic dishes, and tricks on how to use your electric pressure cooker more effectively. With its clear directions and mouth-watering photos, this book entices cooks into the kitchen to create easily executable gluten-free recipes, quashing the misconception that it's impossible to eat well while adhering to dietary restrictions.

> **—Chef Emily Ellyn**, Retro Rad television chef, culinary educator, food writer, and cake genius, as seen on Food Network, Cooking Channel, and HGTV

With easy-to-make recipes from breakfast to dessert and everything in between, *The Gluten-Free Instant Pot Cookbook* has you covered.

> **—Kate McDermott**, author of *Art of the Pie: A Practical Guide to Homemade Crusts, Fillings, and Life* and *Home Cooking with Kate McDermott*

the gluten-free INSTANT POT® COOKBOOK

100 Fast to Fix and
Nourishing Recipes for
All Kinds of Electric
Pressure Cookers

Revised and Expanded Edition

**JANE BONACCI &
SARA DE LEEUW**

HARVARD
COMMON
PRESS

Brimming with creative inspiration, how-to projects, and useful information to enrich your everyday life, Quarto Knows is a favorite destination for those pursuing their interests and passions. Visit our site and dig deeper with our books into your area of interest: Quarto Creates, Quarto Cooks, Quarto Homes, Quarto Lives, Quarto Drives, Quarto Explores, Quarto Gifts, or Quarto Kids.

First Published in 2018 by The Harvard Common Press, an imprint of The Quarto Group,
100 Cummings Center, Suite 265-D, Beverly, MA 01915, USA.
T (978) 282-9590 F (978) 283-2742 QuartoKnows.com

23 22 21 20 19   1 2 3 4 5

ISBN: 978-1-55832-952-2

Digital edition published in 2019
eISBN: 978-1-55832-953-9

Library of Congress Cataloging-in-Publication Data

Bonacci, Jane, author. | De Leeuw, Sara, author.
The gluten-free Instant Pot cookbook : 100 fast-to-fix and nourishing recipes for all kinds of electric pressure cookers /
Jane Bonacci and Sara De Leeuw.
Description: Revised and expanded.
ISBN 9781558329522 (trade pbk.)
1. Gluten-free diet--Recipes. 2. Smart cookers. 3. Electric
  cooking. 4. Cookbooks.
RM237.86 .B663 2018 | 641.5/639311--dc23
LCCN 2018046199

Design and page layout: Laura McFadden Design, Inc.
Photography: Kristin Teig

Printed in China

*To my loving husband James for his unending love, support,
and sense of humor every day. I wouldn't want to take this journey
with anyone else.* —Jane

*To my family and friends for their love and support and
to everyone fighting and dealing with
gluten and other food allergies, this book is for you!* —Sara

CONTENTS

INTRODUCTION

Gluten-Free Cooking with an Electric Pressure Cooker

Hi there! Welcome to the wild and wonderful world of gluten-free pressure cooking. Pressure cooking is all the rage right now. However, if you're one of the millions of people who has a gluten allergy, gluten intolerance, or celiac disease, you may feel severely limited in your choices or as though you can't enjoy the pleasures of using a pressure cooker. We're here to show you this is not the case. Pressure cookers allow you to cook fruits, vegetables, fish, meats, beans, rice, and alternative grains in no time. The possibilities are endless!

In this book, you will find more than 100 recipes that highlight the flavors and tastes of many classic and modern dishes, all without using wheat or other gluten-based ingredients. We know the challenges of eating gluten free, including how difficult it can be to create meals that are both gluten free and delicious. So we took a few favorite gluten-full dishes and a lot of comfort food recipes and did some research. We substituted gluten-free ingredients and then let the pressure cooker work its magic. We were not disappointed! Using a pressure cooker provides new opportunities for meals that all our friends and family (including those with food allergies) can enjoy.

As you know, many commercially produced foods have added gluten. When you are gluten sensitive or have a gluten allergy, you wind up having to make many items from scratch. This can be time-consuming. Having ways to lessen the time needed to get a safe dinner on the table is a big help. Less hands-on time lets you relax and helps make cooking more fun. In our Asian Favorites chapter, you'll still be making a majority of your own sauces, but they all come together quickly. We know you will love the gluten-free options they provide! Having a book like this when we started cooking gluten free would have been a dream—so, please consider this our dream gift to you!

We often hear: "I have a pressure cooker, but I've never taken it out of the box. I'm afraid of it!" We felt the same way! Pressure cookers can be intimidating. Once you muster the courage to try your electric pressure cooker, you'll quickly discover how much fun it is and how it can benefit you in the kitchen. We absolutely love our pressure cookers and rely on them heavily to get nutritious gluten-free dinners on the table and to help prepare healthy lunches for the week.

As with any new appliance, there is a learning curve. If you burned toast the first time you used your toaster, did you give up? No, you kept going, adjusted some buttons, and tried again. It's the same thing with your electric pressure cooker. It gets easier with time and practice. Start simple, and soon you'll be making all kinds of incredible dishes.

Why Use a Pressure Cooker?

There is a certain satisfaction in having dinner simmering away on the stove, filling the house with delicious smells. But what if there were a way to have that same dinner in a fraction of the time? With today's busy schedules and so many people on the go, using an electric pressure cooker can be a game-changer.

Let's walk through some basic information about electric pressure cookers and review some of the tools you'll want to have on hand to be successful.

Pressure cookers have several benefits over more traditional cooking methods. Here are some of the top reasons to use a pressure cooker:

1 Exceptional flavor and nutrition! How food is prepared matters! Pressure cookers create a depth of flavor in your dishes like no other cooking method. They help retain the quality of the foods you cook by preparing them quickly and with very little water. Heat is distributed swiftly, allowing flavor to penetrate into your food more deeply than with traditional cooking. The steam inside the pot allows meats to become moist and succulent and vegetables to retain their crispness, beautiful color, and, most importantly, their flavor. Vitamins and nutrients are better retained in foods cooked with a pressure cooker because they are cooked for a shorter amount of time. Less time means less opportunity for vitamins and minerals to be dissolved away, making food healthier and better for you.

2 Food cooks quickly! In a pressure cooker, the cooking time is greatly reduced. You can cook foods up to 70 percent faster than other conventional methods. This is a handy feature when you're trying to get dinner on the table in a short amount of time. You don't have to spend hours at the stove any longer. Because food is cooked so quickly, it still retains all the richness and natural flavors of foods cooked for hours in the oven. (See above.) You can make a pot of beans, a whole chicken, soups and stews, roasts, and rice so quickly and easily that the pressure cooker will be your new best friend in the kitchen.

3 They are safe! Electric pressure cookers are much safer than your grandmother's (or mother's) pressure cooker. Today's designs have numerous built-in safety features that ensure safe, successful meals without fear of the exploding pressure cookers of yesteryear. The pressure, heating, and sealing functions are all regulated, so you don't have to worry. Lids must be locked in place before pressure builds and won't open until pressure has been released.

4 They use less energy! Electric pressure cookers take far less energy than cooking with multiple pots on your stovetop or hours in your oven. This can be a significant savings. With much less water used in cooking, it is also better for the environment. Because foods are cooked in far less time, less energy is needed to prepare meals. An added bonus? Electric pressure cookers won't heat up the kitchen when you use them.

5 Cleanup is a breeze! Cook in one pot and clean one pot. It doesn't get any easier. Cooking on your stovetop can leave splatters across your counters and walls, resulting in extra mess and more to clean. With an electric pressure cooker, everything is contained, and most of the time, you'll have only one pot and the lid to clean. And less mess means even less time spent in the kitchen. You'll have more time to spend with your kids or doing the things you love.

Finding the Perfect Pressure Cooker

Many brands offer "multifunction" pressure cookers, which can handle a multitude of different tasks. There is no need for several appliances taking up space on your counter. With today's multifunction electric pressure cookers, not only do you get a pressure cooker, but you also get a slow cooker, a rice cooker, a steamer, a warming pot, the ability to sauté and sear, and in some models you can even make your own yogurt. It's an all-in-one package.

With so many different electric pressure cookers on the market today, how do you know which is best for you? The decision about which brand to choose should be based largely on what you like to cook and how you will be using it. Some things to consider are the number of people in your household. If you have a large family, an 8-quart (7.2 L) model (or larger) might be best. If there are just two of you and you don't cook often, a 3- or 4-quart (2.7 or 3.6 L) version might be perfect. All the recipes in this book were written for a 6-quart (5.4 L) pressure cooker, and most often a 6-quart (5.4 L) will give you the most versatility, but choose the one that works best for you and your style of cooking. Something else to take into consideration are the different functions each brand offers. Do you love yogurt? Make sure your model has a yogurt function. (Trust me, I speak from experience on this one. There are three pressure cookers in my house for a reason.) Does your family eat a lot of rice? Explore a brand that has a rice cooker function. Think all those buttons are too complicated for you? Buy one that is rated as exceptionally user-friendly.

How Do Pressure Cookers Work?

A pressure cooker is a sealed pot with a valve that controls the steam and pressure inside the pot. Pressure cookers work by heating liquids in a tightly sealed pot, which creates steam. As the liquid boils, the trapped steam raises the internal cooking temperature past the boiling point of water. The internal temperature of the pot can reach upwards of 250°F (120°C). The higher heat, and conversely higher pressure, forces liquid into the food and cooks it much faster than traditional methods. In fact, foods can be cooked up to 70 percent faster in a pressure cooker. Pressure-cooked foods become moist, juicy, and succulent. Tough fibers break down faster, so inexpensive cuts of meat become fork-tender in a very short amount of time. Dried beans don't need to be soaked for hours, and you can cook healthy, nutritious alternative grains in minutes.

THE PARTS OF A PRESSURE COOKER

Though there are many different brands of electric pressure cookers on the market, they all have similar features. Here are some of the basics you'll find on every model:

Outer Housing Unit or Base: This is what holds the inner cooking pot. The display/control panel will be located on the outside. The control panel is where you will program your pressure cooker to cook. It will have all the function buttons and any preset programs. On the inside of the housing unit is the heating element. This is located at the base of the unit and looks like a ceramic disk. At the center of the heating element is a temperature sensor. The temperature sensor does just that—senses the temperature of your pressure cooker. It will automatically shut off if it senses the temperature inside the pot is too high.

Inner Cooking Pot: This is where the magic happens! Most brands have removable inner pots that are made of stainless steel, ceramic, or aluminum. These are almost all dishwasher safe, and that makes cleanup simple and easy! Always make sure your inner pot is in the housing unit before adding any liquid or ingredients to your pressure cooker. Some inner pots will have a "Max" fill line etched on the inside. This is another safety system for pressure cookers and ensures the food inside doesn't bubble up too far and clog the valves.

Lid: The lid of your pressure cooker is where you'll find the majority of safety features and all the cooking valves.

Pressure Release Valve: This is sometimes called a steam release handle, pressure limit valve, or pressure regulator knob. It is used to control the pressure inside your cooker. Generally, there are two positions for this valve. There is a "sealing" or "pressure" position. This is the position your pressure release valve should be in every time you begin cooking. It will seal in the steam and allow the pressure to build so you can cook food successfully. There is also a "venting" position, used after the cook time is complete to allow the built-up steam to escape. Occasionally these positions are marked on the exterior of the lid, but not always. When you release pressure from a pressure cooker, be aware that very hot steam is being expelled from your machine at a high rate. At no time should you put your face or hands near this steam. Burns from hot steam are quite painful, and we don't want you to get hurt.

Float Pin or Float Valve: This is one of the safety features on a modern electric pressure cooker. A tiny valve located on the lid of your appliance, it resembles a flat nail head. This valve gets pushed up by the steam inside your pot when the unit comes to pressure. The valve helps seal the cooker and prevents the lid from being opened while at pressure. When the float pin drops, it means the majority of pressure has escaped from the pot and you can safely open the lid.

Sealing Ring: Also called a rubber gasket or silicone gasket, this removable ring is found under the lid of your pressure cooker. It's made of stiff food-grade silicone and forms a pressure-tight seal between the lid and the pressure cooker. This is removable, so you can take it out to clean it. Gaskets should be replaced every year or if they develop a thin spot.

THE DISPLAY BUTTONS ON THE CONTROL PANEL

The display buttons on different brands, models, and sizes of electric pressure cookers all have their own functions. Each of those functions makes them unique and special. Many have programs built in for things like soup, grains, meats, eggs, or even cakes. When using these function buttons, the pressure cooker will cook for a specific amount of time at a specific pressure. The time and pressure settings cannot be changed. There is a simple convenience to being able to push a button and walk away. Know, too, that the pressure cooker can't tell what type of food is in the pot. If you use the "Poultry" button for cooking rice because you like how it turns out, no one will ever know.

Every pressure cooker will also have an option for setting the cooking time manually. It may be a button that actually says "Manual," or it might be labeled as something else. Get to know this button on your electric pressure cooker! Many recipes, including all the ones in this book, are written with instructions to "Press Manual and cook for XX minutes." This allows everyone the flexibility to use the same recipes, regardless of the brand or model of pressure cooker you own.

The "Sauté" or "Browning" button allows you to sear food before cooking it. This button works best for searing meats or sautéing vegetables. You can also use this function after cooking to thicken sauces and gravies. Some brands have a "Simmer" option, which you can use in any recipe that doesn't require the higher heat point of sautéing.

There will be a "Cancel/Keep Warm" button. This button will cancel any function currently in progress or simply turn off your pressure cooker. The "Keep Warm" part of the button allows you to keep food inside your cooker warm after the end of the cooking time. Some pressure cookers will let you decide whether you want to keep foods warm or have the cooker automatically shut off at the end of the cooking time. Read your manual to know whether your electric pressure cooker has this option.

Some pressure cookers feature multiple pressure settings, so you can choose to cook at high pressure or low pressure. Usually that setting is changed with + or - buttons located on the control panel.

Your electric pressure cooker will have a display timer that allows you to set the amount of time needed to cook. It will count down once the pot is at pressure and will show you how much cooking time is left before the food is done.

A locking lid is one of the most important safety features of modern electric pressure cookers. The lid cannot be removed while the pot is under pressure. If for some reason something were to go wrong with your pressure cooker, such as the valves were blocked or the electricity were to go out, your lid would remain locked until the pressure inside had decreased enough for the unit to be opened safely. Remember those horror stories about exploding pots and scraping food off the ceiling? This is likely because the lid was forced open on the pressure cooker without properly releasing the inside pressure. Locking lids mean today's electric pressure cookers don't have this problem.

PRESSURE RELEASE METHODS

There are three ways to release the pressure inside your electric pressure cooker: a quick release method, a natural release method, and a combination of the two.

Quick Pressure Release Method, or "QPR": This is when you release all the steam immediately after the cooking time ends. Do this by opening the steam handle to the "venting" or "steam" position and allow all the steam to escape before opening the lid. Depending on what you're cooking, this can take from 1 to 5 minutes.

Natural Pressure Release, or "NPR": This is when you allow your pressure cooker to release built-up pressure naturally. When the cooking time is complete, turn off your appliance and wait until the float pin drops and you can safely open the lid. This can take anywhere from 10 to 30 minutes.

Combination of Natural Pressure Release and Quick Pressure Release: The recipe will call for a natural release for a specific amount of time and then a quick release of the remaining pressure before opening the lid. Example: "When the cook time is finished, allow a 10-minute natural release, then move the handle to the venting position and release any remaining steam. When the float pin drops, unlock the lid and open it carefully."

Regardless of which method your recipe requires, always make sure the float pin has dropped before opening the lid, and always open the lid away from you so you aren't accidentally burned by any residual steam.

Because models and brands vary widely, we strongly recommend you take the time to read the instruction manual that comes with your pressure cooker. It's important to know how your specific model works.

The Hot Water Test

Now that you are familiar with the basic parts of a pressure cooker, how it works, the safety features, and the pressure release methods, it's time to do an initial hot water test. This test is important and will enable you to see how your pressure cooker works. You'll get to see how quickly it comes to pressure, stays at pressure, and then releases pressure. Think of it as a troubleshooting test run. Basically, we're boiling water. We don't know about you, but we would much rather test something with a pot of water than be cooking a full meal and discover there may be a problem. Better to lose a few cups of water than a whole pot of expensive ingredients, right? Doing this test also gives you an opportunity to get comfortable with locking the lid in place, setting your pressure cooker, and using pressure release methods. Ready?

1 First, put the inner pot inside the housing unit. This is a good habit to get into so you don't accidentally pour water (or any other liquids/ingredients) into the housing unit by mistake.

2 Measure 3 cups (705 ml) water and pour it into the inner pot.

3 Inspect the lid to make sure the sealing ring is properly in place, then close and lock the lid.

4 Check to make sure the pressure release valve is closed. This is another good habit to have. Checking the valve every time you close the lid of your pressure cooker will save you from waiting forever for your cooker to come to pressure only to discover the release valve was open and now dinner will take even longer. Yes, we've done this. Many times. It's no fun.

5 Select Manual and set the timer on the control panel to cook for 5 minutes at high pressure.

6 Watch your unit carefully so you can see how it works. Take notes if you wish. It will take from 5 to 10 minutes for your unit to come to pressure. You may be able to hear the water inside begin to boil. You'll also see wisps of steam coming from the float valve. This is normal. The steam is what makes the float valve rise and seal. As you get to know your unit, you'll know when the valve seals because you'll hear a click or you'll notice a distinct lack of noise because the steam is no longer coming out. The timer will start once your unit is at pressure. This doesn't happen immediately after the float valve seals, but will begin within 1 to 2 minutes.

7 When the cook time is over, your unit will beep to let you know it's done. Carefully turn the pressure release valve to the open or venting position (some brands call it the Steam position) and allow the steam to escape. Remember, the steam is very hot and can burn you, so keep your face, hands, and arms away from it. It's also important to note which direction the steam is escaping. You may want to turn your pot so the steam doesn't hit the underside of a cabinet or any wall decorations you may have in your kitchen. If opening the pressure release valve makes you uncomfortable, you can use a pot holder or the handle of a long wooden spoon to gently move it to the open position.

8 Once the pressure and steam are released, you'll hear the float pin drop. On some models you can clearly see it drop back into the recessed position. This means the lid is unlocked and you can now open it safely.

9 Carefully open the lid, tilting it away from you so any residual steam and condensation that has collected under the lid doesn't drip on you or on the counter (or splash onto bare feet. Ouch!). There will always be condensation under the lid after cooking with a pressure cooker. When you open the lid, position it so the water drips back into the pot, instead of going elsewhere.

10 The inner pot will be hot. Use silicone mitts, pot holders, or a kitchen towel to remove it from the housing unit. Measure the amount of water left in the pot. You should see very little difference from the 3 cups (705 ml) water you added in the beginning. You may have lost 1 tablespoon (15 ml) or so, but nothing much above that. In a pressure cooker there is very little liquid lost to evaporation.

11 At this point, if you have chosen a brand that has a Keep Warm setting, you'll see the timer may have begun to count up. Press Cancel or unplug your machine. Different brands/models will allow you to turn off the Keep Warm setting so that when the cook time is over, the pressure cooker simply turns itself off. Either way, be sure to unplug your appliance when you're finished.

That's it! You have successfully done your water test and are ready to create delicious meals for your whole family.

Basic Equipment

Trivet: A trivet or steam rack often comes standard with many electric pressure cookers. This rack keeps food, bowls, and pans elevated off the bottom of the inner cooking pot. This is an essential tool in your pressure-cooking arsenal. We also suggest purchasing a long-legged trivet that will fit in your pressure cooker. This is useful for several of our pot-in-pot recipes, as it allows more food underneath while still keeping another pot balanced safely above.

Steamer Basket: Generally speaking, when we say "steamer basket," we are referring to a collapsible basket made of stainless steel with overlapping side leaves that can be expanded to fit inside most 6- or 8-quart (5.4 or 7.2 L) pressure cookers. It has a colander-type basket and has feet, so it can be used to hold vegetables or proteins over boiling water to steam them. The center post, which occasionally has a ring on the end of it, can be used to help lift the basket from the inner pot. The center post is also removable, which makes it perfect for steaming larger vegetables like whole artichokes or spaghetti squash. You can find steamer baskets made of silicone or smaller baskets that double as strainers and come with lift handles that also fit easily inside most 6-quart (5.4 L) or larger pressure cookers.

Instant-Read Thermometer: (We recommend Thermapen from ThermoWorks.) An instant-read thermometer helps you check to ensure larger cuts of meats have been cooked to a safe internal temperature. It is also beneficial in ensuring your yogurt (if your pressure cooker has that function) has reached the proper temperature.

A 7 x 3-Inch (18 x 7.6 cm) Springform Pan or Push Pan: This is great to use for cheesecakes and lasagna. The sides of a springform pan expand and then buckle closed. It has a detachable bottom, which makes removing cheesecakes simple and easy. A push pan (we like Fat Daddio's) also has a removable bottom, but the sides of the pan are solid, so removing things like lasagna is nearly effortless.

A 7 x 3-Inch (18 x 7.6 cm) Round Cake Pan: We use this pan a lot. If you can afford only one additional pan, make it this one. It's useful for cakes, spinach dip, frittatas, meatloaf, and pot-in-pot rice. If necessary, this pan can also be used for lasagna, but you will have difficulty removing your food.

A 6-Cup (1440 g) Bundt Pan: This half-size Bundt pan (we love Nordic Ware) fits perfectly inside most 6-quart (5.4 L) electric pressure cookers. Use it for cakes or bread pudding!

Small 4-Ounce (112 g) Mason Jars: These are sometimes called quilted jelly jars and are perfect for making individual-size cheesecakes or desserts.

Flat Wooden Spatula or Turner: This utensil helps scrape any browned bits off the bottom of the pot when you sauté your food and easily breaks up clumps when cooking ground meat.

A 1½ -Quart (1.4 L) Round Ceramic Casserole Dish without Handles: This is a great dish to have. It can double as a rice dish for pot-in-pot meals. It will fit a batch of Spinach Artichoke Dip (page 50) perfectly and fits seamlessly inside a 6-quart (5.4 L) pressure cooker.

Additional Silicone Rings: You will need to replace your sealing ring (sealing gasket) at least once a year. Thankfully they are not expensive. Some people have different colored gaskets that they switch out regularly for use when making sweet dishes versus savory dishes. The gaskets do tend to pick up odors, and who wants a cheesecake that smells like spaghetti and meatballs?

Aluminum Foil Sling: One of the best tools you will use with your pressure cooker is an aluminum sling. It will help you lift pans in and out of the pressure cooker with ease. The great thing about an aluminum sling? It is not expensive and you can use it over and over again. I keep mine in the same drawer as my plastic storage bags and parchment paper. First, tear off a sheet of aluminum foil about 24 inches (61 cm) long and lay it out on the kitchen table. Fold it lengthwise evenly into thirds, much like you were folding a piece of paper to put in an envelope. Run your hands over the edges to flatten it. Center the pan you want to lift in the middle of your newly created sling. Fold the edges up around the pan and bring the ends together. Twist the ends together to create a handle. Now you can safely place pans inside your pressure cooker without spilling the contents and, more importantly, you can lift hot pans out of the pressure cooker without burning your fingers. Some people like to create two slings for extra support on each side of the baking dish.

Silicone Pinch Mitts: Small, heat-resistant oven mitts designed to protect your hands and fingers from the hot inner cooking pot, these mitts allow you to grip the edges of the pot without getting burned. Most come with a textured grip surface to reduce the risk of slipping.

Retriever Tongs: These are different than traditional kitchen tongs. Retriever tongs are great for taking a very hot dish out of a container. They are designed to clip and lift the inner pot or steamer basket from your pressure cooker. They are also useful for taking hot plates from the oven or microwave without having to touch them.

Jar Lifter Tongs: This is a tool used often in canning. It is essential for lifting hot jars out of a water bath canner. It is also very useful for getting individual jars of cheesecake out of your pressure cooker.

Special Equipment and Accessories

Immersion Blender: This is a powerful stick blender. It is lightweight with sharp blades, and you can use it to blend foods right in your pressure cooker. You can mash potatoes, blend sauces, process hummus, and more. It usually comes with a whisk attachment and some kind of bowl or beaker, which also makes blending sauce or pesto easy and convenient.

An 8 x 4-Inch (20.3 x 10.2 cm) Loaf Pan: Instant Pot has a springform silicone loaf pan that fits beautifully inside their 6-quart (5.4 L) electric pressure cookers. It's handy to bake more traditional meatloaf or quick breads.

Kitchen Scale: We recommend the OXO Good Grips Food Scale with an 11-pound (5 kg) capacity. This is especially important for your gluten-free baking needs. This scale will allow you to measure in both U.S. and metric increments. It has a zero function, which allows you to tare the scale with a bowl or other container before measuring so you'll have accurately measured ingredients every time.

Tips for Using Your Pressure Cooker Successfully

Always read the instruction manual that comes with your pressure cooker. It may seem boring or unnecessary, but the manuals are written for a reason. It's critical to your success to know your pressure cooker's strengths and limitations.

Never use your electric pressure cooker on the stovetop. There is a difference between a stove-top pressure cooker and an electric pressure cooker. Electric pressure cookers are meant to be stand-alone counter appliances. We've heard of people accidently melting their electric pressure cooker because they put it on a stovetop and a burner was mistakenly turned on underneath. For the purposes of this book, we focus solely on countertop electric pressure cookers.

Be aware of recipes and timing. This is imperative to keep in mind when planning your meals. Cooking in a pressure cooker is fast, but it does take time to put together. Always read through the entire recipe, sometimes twice. There is nothing worse than starting a recipe only to realize you are missing an essential ingredient. Consider the time it takes to prep your ingredients, then the time it takes for your pressure cooker to come to pressure. The same way an oven must preheat, pressure cookers need time to heat up and begin to build steam and pressure to cook your food. Also factor the total recipe cooking time and any specific pressure release time into your planning. A "3-minute" recipe might actually take 20 to 25 minutes depending on the temperature of your ingredients and how much liquid is in your pressure cooker.

Altitude can make a difference! Because pressure cookers are built on the principle of boiling water to create steam, it's important to know that water boils at lower temperatures at higher elevations. For pressure cookers, shorter cooking times at a higher elevation is generally not a problem, but for longer cooking times or specific foods like grains or beans, you may need to make adjustments. A good, basic rule to follow is to add 5 percent more cooking time for each 1,000 feet (305 m) after 3,000 feet (915 m) above sea level. So if you live at 4,000 feet (1220 m), you would add 10 percent; at 5,000 feet (1524 m), add 15 percent; and so on. If you aren't sure, always use a food thermometer to help determine the temperature of your food. If you need to make adjustments from there, then you can do so safely. *Note:* All the recipes in this book were tested at or near sea level.

Always ensure you have enough liquid in the inner pot to bring it to pressure. The minimum amount of liquid will vary depending on the brand of electric pressure cooker. Generally speaking, this is at least 1 cup (235 ml) of liquid, but check your owner's manual and always use tested recipes. Some recipes may call for less liquid because the food you are cooking releases a lot of water during the cooking process. An example is our Sweet Spiced Applesauce (page 207). It only requires ¼ cup (60 ml) of liquid.

Do not overfill your pressure cooker. Pressure cookers require space for steam to build pressure and cook properly. A basic guideline is no more than two-thirds full for most recipes and half full for foods such as beans and grains, as they tend to expand and foam during cooking. Overfilling a pot can also create hazards and clog your vent pipes and valves. If your vents and valves get dirty, you'll need to clean them so your cooker can properly come to pressure.

If you hear popping noises, don't worry. This is common. Popping noises happen when the heating unit goes from one temperature to another and can happen occasionally if the bottom of your inner pot is wet. Be sure to dry it completely before starting to cook.

Some steam coming from the release valve is normal. Small wisps of steam will happen as the unit is coming to pressure before the float valve seals. However, if large plumes of steam continue for more than 2 minutes, check the valve to make sure it is set to sealing, not venting. If that doesn't fix the problem, you may have food debris on the float pin that is blocking the valve from sealing. Simply clean it according to your manufacturer's instructions and try again.

Brown meats or vegetables first, then deglaze the pot for more flavor. Many recipes will ask you to add oil or butter to the inner cooking pot and then brown or sauté an ingredient. Add the food in small batches and evenly brown the food on all sides. Remove the food to a serving plate or bowl, then use water, stock, or whatever liquid is specified in the recipe to loosen up and remove those delicious, cooked-on food particles left on the bottom of the pan. This is a great flavor enhancer for your dishes.

Follow instructions for thickening sauces. Many recipes designed for pressure cookers call for thickening the sauces and gravies after cooking. This is because pressure cookers use liquid to create steam and that liquid needs to be thin. Adding flour is a common way to thicken that flavorful cooking liquid in your pressure cooker, but for those who are gluten free, that is not an option. Instead, we use alternative thickeners. A cornstarch slurry (a mixture of cornstarch and water), arrowroot powder, or tapioca starch are good options for use in a pressure cooker. If your recipe calls for white beans, you can also blend ¼ cup (60 g) beans with ¼ cup (60 ml) of the cooking liquid into a bean slurry and use it to thicken soups and stews. Simmering the sauces until they're reduced is another option.

In this book, we'll give you guides to help if you are new to a gluten-free diet or only cook occasionally, help with setting up your kitchen, recommendations for gluten-free ingredients, and information you can use in all your gluten-free baking and cooking. Everyone, regardless of diet, can be a part of the pressure cooker revolution!

So, whether you are new to pressure cooking, new to gluten-free living, or are already an expert and simply want new recipes, we've got you covered. Come on, let's get cooking!

A Gluten-Free Kitchen and Home

How to Go Gluten Free

If you are new to gluten-free eating, it can be daunting. Where do you start? Which foods are safe? How do you avoid gluten when everything seems to contain something forbidden? Just know that it does get easier and you will conquer the challenge.

Depending on the severity of the gluten sensitivity, some families have to keep an entirely gluten-free kitchen. Others can get by with designating specific areas of the kitchen and pantry for gluten-free use, especially if they are only cooking gluten-free foods occasionally for friends or visiting family members.

CREATING A GLUTEN-FREE KITCHEN

If the entire family is going to be eating gluten free, the first thing you need to do is clean out your kitchen (don't forget the refrigerator) and get rid of your gluten-full foods. Then hit the grocery store and restock your kitchen.

If you are worried about how to shop for groceries, stay to the periphery of the store, where they stock the fresh produce, meats, and dairy. Focusing on those will give you the most options for foods that are naturally safe for your entire family. Rice and potatoes are good, filling options to accompany main courses.

CREATING A DUAL-USE KITCHEN

In the instance where you can have a dual-use kitchen, shared equipment needs to be washed thoroughly after every use. Just make sure you don't use the same sponges or cloths to wash the gluten-free pans and dishes. For those items that cannot be fully submerged in water, like electrical appliances (toaster, panini press, toaster oven, etc.), it is safer to buy a second one to avoid cross-contamination.

Designating a single area for storing all your gluten-free food and cooking items will make it much easier for you and your gluten-free family members to know where their food is. If you have little ones, putting a strip of brightly colored duct tape on their containers of food can help them know which ones are theirs. This will keep them safe if they are looking for snacks when you are not around to supervise.

Equipment that is porous has to be separated, including cutting boards, storage containers, and wooden utensils. Stores sell sets of colored plastic cutting boards that will help you designate a specific color to be used with all gluten-free preparations. Buy a second toaster in a bright color so you can see which one to use right away. You can set up a cute pitcher and keep your gluten-free-specific mixing spoons and spatulas

there. Buy a second set of food storage containers with different color tops and keep them on their own shelf.

CAN YOU USE THE SAME PRESSURE COOKER FOR REGULAR AND GLUTEN-FREE COOKING?

Sensitivity to gluten varies from person to person, from mild to extreme. But for people with celiac disease, even the slightest cross-contamination can cause illness. There are so many crevices and surfaces to clean on the equipment that it is nearly impossible to remove every single grain of gluten, and it is much safer to use different equipment than to risk your family's health. If you will be cooking both regular and gluten-free foods for your family, we recommend you have two machines with one that is dedicated for gluten-free cooking only.

To help you tell them apart, use colored sealing rings and decals to indicate which machine is designated for gluten-free cooking. The Instant Pot Lux version also comes in several colors to make it even easier—find them on the Instant Pot website, https://instantpot.com/portfolio_entries/lux-series.

Special Ingredient Considerations

THICKENERS

When we want to thicken a sauce, we naturally reach for all-purpose flour, but when you are gluten free this is no longer an option. Thankfully, we are lucky that alternative thickeners are easy to find and make wonderful substitutions.

Cornstarch (or cornflour in the UK): Cornstarch is the most efficient gluten-free thickener and our top choice. If you cannot have corn (sometimes found in conjunction with gluten sensitivities), choose one of the other starches below. Cornstarch must be dissolved in water before adding to cooking liquids to avoid clumps. It must also be brought to a full boil to activate it and then simmered for a few minutes to cook off any raw flavor.

Tapioca starch (also called tapioca flour): Tapioca thickens at a much lower temperature, so keep the liquid just below a boil and do not stir for a long time if using this starch. Tapioca starch/flour is often carried at higher-end grocery stores in the baking aisle. If you cannot find it, it is readily available online.

Potato starch (not potato flour): Potato starch is very different from potato flour and cannot be used in the same way (especially important in baking applications). It is often sold in the same area as other starches in the baking aisle. Potato starch thickens very quickly with little to no flavor, making it great for a last-minute addition to thicken sauces. Do not cook too long or it may break down.

Arrowroot: This is an option for those who cannot have potatoes, corn, or nightshades in their diet. Arrowroot comes from the root of the plant; it is ground exceptionally finely, giving you extremely smooth sauces. Use at the very end of cooking and take off the heat once the sauce is at your desired thickness.

OATS

Oats can be confusing. Some people swear they can eat them and others have a reaction to them. Oats are often grown beside gluten crops and processed on the same equipment, frequently causing cross-contamination issues. There are a few vendors that sell certified gluten-free oats, such as Bob's Red Mill. Always look for a gluten-free certification and if you have any questions, contact the manufacturer directly.

SAUSAGE, HAM, AND SOME TURKEY

Most commercial sausages contain fillers that commonly include gluten ingredients. If you have a reputable butcher, you can ask them about what they put in their house-made sausages. If you want to buy sausages at the grocery store, some readily available brands that have gluten-free versions are Aidells, Jones Dairy Farm, and Boar's Head (read the labels). Commercially produced hams and turkeys often have gluten ingredients in the brine and injected liquids. Likewise, be careful with presliced and packaged deli meats— many will contain gluten ingredients. Always read the packaging carefully, look for a gluten-free certification, and if you have any questions, contact the manufacturer.

SOY SAUCE

In the United States and elsewhere in the world, wheat is added to soy sauce (and other products made with it). It is used as a flavor enhancer and found in many foods. Tamari is another form of soy sauce and often is gluten free, but it is not guaranteed without certification. Look for gluten-free brands, clearly marked on the front label. You can substitute gluten-free soy sauce for regular in any recipe. If you cannot have soy, try coconut aminos, an excellent soy-free replacement.

DISTILLED SPIRITS

This is one of the most debated subjects in the gluten-free world. You will hear people strongly arguing on either side of the issue. The process of distillation destroys gluten, resulting in products that fall below the industry standard of 20 ppm. However, there are some people who may still react even below the standard. Another culprit may be because some distillers add caramel coloring to their alcohols, and these colorings often contain gluten ingredients. If you are cooking for someone with celiac or who is highly reactive, it is safer to use a grain-free alcohol like potato vodka for flavoring. Adding a teaspoon of brown sugar will make it a decent substitute for grain alcohol.

WINE

Wine is considered gluten free, but there may be a couple of gotchas for the most sensitive folks. Because it comes from grapes and not grain, it tests to well below the standard of 20 ppm. But there may be issues with added coloring or flavoring—usually found in dessert wines or wine coolers—so it pays to avoid those.

There are two primary sources of contamination in the wine industry: the caulking agents used with wooden aging barrels and the fining agents used to clarify wines. Some wooden barrels are sealed with a wheat-based caulk. Even though the chances of a reaction are slim, if you are having issues, look for winemakers who use stainless steel tanks. A less likely cause of a reaction could be the fining agents, particles winemakers use to make wines crystal clear. Reactions because of fining agents are rare, but if you are one of the few, you can contact the winery and ask what they use to clarify their wines.

In cooking, wine is often used to add flavor and interest to recipes. If you are hosting guests, feel free to ask them about their level of sensitivity and, in this case, whether they drink wine. If you are unsure how reactive your family or guests may be, you can always use stock or water and leave out the wine.

Where to Find Gluten-Free Products

We are lucky that gluten-free products are much more readily available today than they were even five years ago. Some stores have a dedicated area, but usually you will find the gluten-free products interspersed with gluten-full items on the shelves. Psyllium can sometimes be found in the health section, under colon health. If your local shops don't carry everything you are looking for, you can order most things online, either directly at the manufacturer's site or on Amazon.com.

Following the recipes and product recommendations we give you in this book will help you make healthier, safer choices. When you and your family are hungry and need a meal, you will appreciate the speed of today's pressure cookers. You can have a meal on the table in a fraction of the time it takes to make many dishes in the oven or on the stove.

Our Recommended Flour Blend and Other Gluten-Free Flour Blends

When you are baking or cooking certain recipes, you will need to use a gluten-free all-purpose flour. If you will be baking a lot, making your own blend in bulk will save you money. If you are only using it occasionally, feel free to use a store-bought brand. Some of our favorites are Bob's Red Mill Gluten Free 1-to-1 Baking Flour, Pamela's All-Purpose Gluten-Free Flour, King Arthur Gluten-Free All-Purpose Flour, Cup4Cup Gluten-Free Flour Blend, and Authentic Foods' Gluten-Free Classical Blend.

In addition to gluten-free flours, a blend needs starches to give structure and lift to your baked goods. Starches are nearly always included, but it is not a given that the blend you buy includes gums or psyllium husk powder. Gums help hold your baked goods together and keep them from crumbling. If your commercial blend includes xanthan gum (or guar gum), reduce the amount called for in recipes by half. If you are sensitive to gums, you can use psyllium husk powder for the same purpose. Just use double the amount. So if the recipe calls for 1 teaspoon xanthan gum, replace that with 2 teaspoons psyllium husk powder.

To make it easier for you, we have included our favorite all-purpose blend to use in any baking and cooking recipes, both from this book and from other sources.

All-Purpose Gluten-Free Flour Blend

When you are baking or making recipes that call for flour, having a gluten-free blend already made and available is helpful. Use 120 grams of the blend for every 1 cup of flour called for in any recipe. This blend does not contain any dairy, nuts, or gums, making it very versatile. You can use it in everything calling for flour.

Yield 1.8 pounds, or about 6 cups (800 g)

280 g (9.9 ounces, or 2¼ cups) sweet rice flour (not white rice flour)

280 g (9.9 ounces, or 2 ¼ cups) brown or white rice flour

120 g (4.2 ounces, or 1 cup plus 4¾ teaspoons) tapioca flour/starch

120 g (4.2 ounces, or ¾ cup) potato starch (not potato flour)

1 Whisk the ingredients together and store in a large food-safe plastic bin. Secure the lid on the container and shake vigorously to distribute all the ingredients evenly.

2 Gluten-free flours tend to settle and sometimes separate while sitting, so always shake the container well before measuring for each baking project.

1
BEGUILING BREAKFASTS

We always hear, "Breakfast is the most important meal of the day," and it's true. It puts fuel in our tank and wakes up our brain, giving us the energy we need to be effective and successful every day.

Steel-cut oats take a really long time to cook on the stove, but when you use your electric pressure cooker, they can easily be made for hungry family members on school days. They hold their texture and stay chewy, the perfect way to wake up on cold days. Just be sure to use a certified gluten-free brand.

Frittatas are an Italian omelet-like egg preparation made in a pan inside the pressure cooker and quiche is the French version. Utilizing the steam of the pressure cooker, they bake into a soufflé-like texture. With their tender and delicate perfection, they make a lovely centerpiece for any brunch or breakfast.

Grits are a classic in the American South, and our version is packed with savory flavors of sausage, cheese, and jalapeño. This is another dish guaranteed to fill up the hungriest folks at your table.

If you are looking for a healthy meal on busy mornings, try our Sweet Potato and Egg Caribbean Breakfast Burritos (page 40) or the Maple-Kissed Millet Porridge (page 39). They are filled with delicious flavors and ingredients, and you can get them on the table quickly. Starting your day with a wholesome breakfast will make every day brighter!

Recipes

Greek Yogurt with Fresh Fruit

GLUTEN FREE • VEGETARIAN • SOY FREE • NUT FREE • EGG FREE

Making yogurt is one of the most popular functions of the new electric pressure cookers, but not all brands and models have a cycle to do it automatically. Make sure your model has a yogurt button if you will be making yogurt often. Using whole milk will give you the creamiest yogurt and you can make 18 servings for about $4.00—what a savings!

If you have a machine without a yogurt button, you can find directions at www.thefeventmama.com/ pressure-cooker-yogurt to guide you in making yogurt in your pressure cooker.

For the yogurt starter, use yogurt with live and active cultures only; this will be listed in the ingredients on the packaging. A good choice is Fage Total 0%.

Yield About 18 servings

For the yogurt

1 gallon (4 L) whole or 2% ultra-pasteurized milk

2 tablespoons (30 g) yogurt starter, such as Fage Total 0%

For serving

Fresh berries or other fruit

Gluten-free granola (optional)

Sterilize Your Pressure Cooker

1 Place the inner pot in the pressure cooker. Add 3 cups (705 ml) water to the pot, lock the lid in place, and make sure the steam release handle is in the sealing position. Cook on high pressure for 5 minutes, then do a quick release of the steam. When the pressure valve drops, unlock the lid and open it carefully. Pour out the water, dry the inner pot, and set aside to cool.

Yogurt

1 Pour the milk into the cooled inner pot, place in the pressure cooker, and cover with a glass lid (you will not be using pressure, so you don't need the standard lid). Press the Yogurt button and then the Adjust button until it reads "Boil." While this cycle is happening, stir the milk a few times, making sure to replace the lid each time. This cycle will take about 45 minutes.

2 When the cycle has ended, use an instant-read thermometer (we like the Thermapen from ThermoWorks) to be sure it has reached at least 180°F (82°C). If it is too low, use the Sauté (on low) feature, whisking constantly, until the temperature is between 180°F and 200°F (82°C and 93°C). Remove the inner pot and set it in your kitchen sink, far from the faucet. Fill the sink to halfway up the sides of the pot with cold water (don't let it splash into the milk) and cool the yogurt to 95°F to 110°F (35°C to 43°C), whisking to speed the process. This will take about 10 minutes. Remove the pot from the sink and wipe the exterior completely dry.

3 When the mixture has cooled, remove 1 cup (235 ml) of the milk and place it in a bowl. Add the starter, whisking to combine. Whisk this tempered starter back into the milk, whisking until it is evenly distributed throughout. Return the dried inner pot to your pressure cooker, cover with the lid, and press the Yogurt button, then the Adjust button until it says "Normal." Set the time for 8 to 12 hours; the longer the yogurt incubates, the more tart it will be. We find 10 hours is a good starting point.

4 When the time is up, lift out the inner pot, cover with plastic wrap, and place in the refrigerator. Leave it undisturbed for 6 hours to thoroughly cool.

Strain the Yogurt

1 Set a very large bowl on the counter and set up a draining station using cheesecloth, muslin, or coffee filters in as big a wire strainer as you can find. You can set up more than one strainer/bowl if you have the space in your refrigerator, or make a half batch, which is easier to strain. Pour the chilled milk into the strainer, cover loosely with plastic wrap, and transfer to the refrigerator. Leave for at least 2 hours to drain off most of the liquid and thicken the yogurt.

2 Pour the yogurt into Mason jars for storage in the refrigerator. Be sure to save some of the strained yogurt to use as your starter for your next batch. The yogurt will keep in the refrigerator up to 3 weeks.

To Serve

1 Spoon some of the yogurt into bowls, top with your choice of fresh fruit and a little granola (if using), and serve for a healthy and filling breakfast.

Creamy Steel-Cut Oatmeal with Apple Raisin Compote

GLUTEN FREE • VEGETARIAN • SOY FREE • NUT FREE • EGG FREE

This breakfast treat is a cross between old-fashioned oatmeal and an apple pie with a hit of cinnamon to wake up your taste buds. Warm and comforting, it is the perfect way to start your day.

When you cook with regular steel-cut oats, you run the risk of cross-contamination due to how they are grown and processed. But if you buy certified gluten-free steel-cut oats, you can eat them with confidence. Bob's Red Mill offers gluten-free oats that can be found at grocery stores and are also available for purchase online at www.bobsredmill.com.

Yield 4 to 6 servings

For the compote

1 tart apple, such as Granny Smith

1 sweet apple, such as Golden Delicious

3 tablespoons (30 g) golden raisins (optional)

½ cup (120 ml) orange juice or apple juice

2 teaspoons (10 ml) freshly squeezed lemon juice

2 tablespoons (30 g) brown sugar

2 tablespoons (30 ml) maple syrup

½ teaspoon ground cinnamon

½ teaspoon gluten-free vanilla extract

½ teaspoon fresh lemon zest

For the oatmeal

Butter, for greasing

3 cups (705 ml) water

2 cups (470 ml) milk or dairy-free milk of your choice

2 cups (320 g) steel-cut oats (do not use regular rolled or instant oats)

Pinch of kosher or fine sea salt

Compote

1 Peel and core the apples and cut into small chunks. Place in a saucepan. Add the raisins, orange juice, lemon juice, brown sugar, maple syrup, cinnamon, vanilla, and lemon zest. Stir to combine. Cook over medium heat, stirring occasionally, until the apples are fork tender and the liquid is syrupy. Transfer the compote to a bowl and set aside.

Oatmeal

1 Lightly butter the bottom and lower sides of the inner pot to help prevent sticking. Add the water, milk, oats, and salt, in this order but do *not* stir. Close and lock the lid, making sure the steam release handle is in the sealing position. Cook on high pressure for 9 minutes. When it is finished, release the pressure naturally, which will take about 15 minutes. Turn the steam release handle to venting, releasing any remaining steam. Unlock the lid and open it carefully.

2 Scoop the oatmeal into bowls and top with a spoonful or two of the fruit compote. Serve immediately.

Crustless Quiche Lorraine

GLUTEN FREE • SOY FREE • NUT FREE

Quiche Lorraine is quintessential French food. Often served for lunch or brunch, it is surprisingly rich and light at the same time. When served with a lightly dressed green salad, it makes the perfect meal. One bite and you will be instantly transported to the Musée d'Orsay in Paris, enjoying a lovely meal surrounded by the astonishing art of the Impressionists. Très bien!

Yield About 4 servings

Once the quiche has cooked, you may want to put it under the broiler for a few minutes to lightly brown the top.

To store: Refrigerate, covered, for up to two days.

4 strips thick-cut gluten-free bacon, chopped

½ small onion, thinly sliced, rings separated

6 large eggs

½ cup (120 ml) heavy cream

½ cup (120 ml) half-and-half

½ teaspoon kosher or fine sea salt

¼ teaspoon freshly ground black pepper

¼ teaspoon ground nutmeg (optional)

1 cup (120 g) shredded Gruyère or Swiss cheese

¼ cup (25 g) grated Parmesan cheese

Finely chopped scallions or chives

1 cup (235 ml) water for the bottom of the pot

1 Spray a 7-inch (18 cm) round baking pan or push pan with nonstick vegetable spray and line the bottom with a sheet of parchment. Set a square of foil and an aluminum sling (see page 18) next to the pan.

2 Press Sauté and place the bacon pieces in the inner pot of your electric pressure cooker. Cook, stirring often, until crispy. Use a slotted spoon to transfer the bacon to a paper towel–lined plate. Remove all but 1 tablespoon (15 ml) of the fat.

3 Add the onions to the pot and cook, stirring, until softened and transparent, about 4 minutes. Transfer to the plate and wipe out the pot. Press Cancel. Place a trivet in the bottom of the inner pot and pour in 1 cup (235 ml) water.

4 In a bowl, whisk the eggs, cream, half-and-half, salt, pepper, and nutmeg (if using) until smooth. Stir in the Gruyère cheese, cooked bacon, and

onions. Pour into the prepared pan and sprinkle the Parmesan over the top. Cover with the foil, crimping the edges around the pan. Use the sling to lift the pan onto the trivet.

5 Close and lock the lid, making sure the steam release handle is in the sealing position. Cook on high pressure for 20 minutes. When it is finished, release the pressure naturally for 10 minutes, then quick release any remaining pressure. Unlock the lid and open it carefully.

6 Use the sling to lift the pan out of the pot and place on a wire cooling rack. If there is any water pooled on top, use a paper towel to absorb it. Carefully remove the foil from the pan. Let it cool for about 15 minutes, then cut into slices, and sprinkle with the scallions or chives. Serve warm or at room temperature.

Sausage and Jalapeño Cheese Grits

GLUTEN FREE • SOY FREE • NUT FREE • EGG FREE

On a trip to Georgia, we were treated to our host's famous grits. Each morning, we would head to the kitchen and watch as he proudly made his specialty. This recipe is packed with flavor from sausage, jalapeño peppers, and cheese. Healthy and filling, these grits gave us energy for our days of sightseeing in the beautiful wooded back roads of Georgia.

Many folks will resort to using quick grits to save time on busy days. With today's electric pressure cookers, you can enjoy the superior flavor of long-cooked stone-ground or coarse-ground grits prepared in a fraction of the time.

Yield 4 servings

3 tablespoons (45 ml) olive or vegetable oil, divided

½ pound (227 g) raw mild Homemade Sausage, see opposite page

¼ cup (40 g) finely chopped onion

½ jalapeño pepper, finely minced, or more to taste

1 cup (140 g) stone-ground grits (*not* instant grits)

3 cups (705 ml) cool water

1½ cups (355 ml) half-and-half or heavy cream

2 teaspoons (12 g) kosher or fine sea salt

1 cup (120 g) shredded cheddar cheese, divided

1 Press Sauté and heat 1 tablespoon (15 ml) of the oil in the inner pot of your electric pressure cooker. When it is hot, add the sausage and cook, stirring often, until completely browned. Break up any clumps that form, keeping the pieces small and easy to eat. Add the onion and jalapeño and stir to combine. Cook for about 3 minutes to soften the vegetables. Transfer to a bowl and set aside.

2 Add the remaining 2 tablespoons (30 ml) oil and the grits to the inner pot and cook, stirring often, for 1 minute, until the oil has been absorbed and the grits are lightly toasted. Stir in the water, half-and-half, and salt. Press Cancel.

3 Close and lock the lid, making sure the steam release handle is in the sealing position. Cook on high pressure for 10 minutes. When it is finished, release the pressure naturally for 10 minutes, then turn the steam release handle to venting, releasing any remaining steam. Unlock the lid and open it carefully.

4 Whisk the grits until smooth. If they are too thick and heavy, add a tablespoon (15 ml) milk or more as needed to get a smooth, creamy texture. Stir the sausage mixture into the grits. Add half the cheese and stir until it is melted. Scoop into serving bowls and top with remaining cheese. Serve immediately.

Homemade Sausage

GLUTEN FREE • DAIRY FREE • SOY FREE • NUT FREE • EGG FREE

Sausage often contains gluten fillers, but by making it yourself, you can control the purity of the ingredients, the percentage of fat, and the seasonings. Once you've tried this sausage, we doubt you will ever use store-bought again.

Yield 2½ pounds (1138 g)

2 teaspoons (12 g) minced parsley

1 teaspoon kosher or fine sea salt

1 teaspoon rubbed sage

1 teaspoon dried thyme

1 teaspoon gluten-free chili powder (optional)

1 teaspoon freshly ground black pepper

1 teaspoon dried basil leaves

1 teaspoon dried oregano

⅓ cup (55 g) grated onion

2½ pounds (1.1 kg) ground pork or a combination of ground pork and ground turkey

1 Combine the herbs and spices in a small bowl.

2 Place the onion and meat in a large bowl. Add the seasoning blend and mix together with your hands until evenly distributed.

3 Divide the mixture into two or three sections and roll each one into a log. Wrap the logs individually in plastic wrap and refrigerate overnight or freeze for longer storage. When ready to use, slice into patties or use in bulk.

Cheesy Poblano Frittata

GLUTEN FREE • VEGETARIAN
• SOY FREE • NUT FREE

Frittatas are a quick and easy breakfast, brunch, or midweek dinner option. The cumin and peppers add flavor and a little heat, which takes this in a Southwestern direction. You can pass hot sauce at the table if you have guests who like spicier foods. Serving a tossed green salad alongside makes a healthy, light meal.

If you are using a springform or push pan, wrap the outside of the pan with foil to ensure the liquid remains inside the pan. The foil on top also helps keep most of the steam from collecting in the bottom of the pan.

Yield 4 servings

To add some color to the cooked frittata, put it under the broiler before you cut into it.

1 tablespoon (15 ml) olive or vegetable oil

¼ cup (40 g) finely chopped onion

2 poblano peppers, seeded and finely chopped

1 red bell pepper, cored, seeded, and finely chopped

1 tablespoon (1 g) finely minced fresh cilantro leaves, plus more for garnish

½ teaspoon ground cumin

6 large eggs

1 cup (235 ml) half-and-half

½ teaspoon kosher or fine sea salt

¼ teaspoon freshly ground black pepper

1 cup (120 g) shredded Colby or cheddar cheese, divided

For the cooking pot

1½ cups (355 ml) water

1 Spray a 7 x 3-inch (18 x 7.6 cm) round baking pan with nonstick vegetable cooking spray. Tear off a piece of foil large enough to cover the pan and spray one side.

2 Press Sauté on your electric pressure cooker. Add the oil to the inner pot. When hot, add the onion and peppers. Cook, stirring often, until softened, about 5 minutes. Stir in the cilantro and cumin. Press Cancel. Transfer the vegetables to a bowl.

3 Wipe out the inner pot, return it to the pressure cooker, place a trivet in the bottom, and pour in the water.

4 In a bowl, whisk together the eggs, half-and-half, salt, and pepper. Stir in the cooked onions and peppers and ¾ cup (90 g) of the cheese. Pour into the prepared baking pan. Sprinkle the remaining

cheese over the top. Cover with the foil, sprayed side down, crimping it around the edges of the pan. Use a sling (see page 18) to lower it into the inner pot.

5 Close and lock the lid, making sure the steam release handle is in the sealing position. Cook on high pressure for 20 minutes. When it is finished, release the pressure naturally for 10 minutes, then turn the steam release handle to venting, releasing any remaining steam. Unlock the lid and open it carefully.

6 With the sling, lift the pan out of the pot. Set on a wire cooling rack and carefully remove the foil. Use a paper towel to pat any excess liquid off the top of the frittata.

7 Cut into wedges, and sprinkle the top with additional cilantro if desired. Serve hot.

Savory Breakfast Bread Pudding

GLUTEN FREE • VEGETARIAN OPTION • SOY FREE • NUT FREE

Bread puddings seem to be a thing of the past when you can no longer eat gluten. But improvements in store-bought breads and those made from scratch give us the opportunity to enjoy this wonderful breakfast treat again. Serve this with a fresh fruit salad for a lovely brunch with friends. And if you have a sweet tooth, don't miss our Apple Cinnamon Raisin Bread Pudding (page 192), another favorite!

Yield 4 servings

Notes: Once you remove the foil from the cooked bread pudding you may want to slide the pan under the broiler to add color and crispiness to the top.

This can be made a day ahead. Cover and refrigerate. Reheat gently, covered, in the oven.

1 tablespoon (15 ml) olive or vegetable oil

8 ounces (227 g) uncooked Homemade Sausage (page 35; omit for vegetarian)

1 cup (160 g) finely diced onion

½ cup (75 g) finely diced red bell pepper

6 large eggs

½ cup (120 ml) half-and-half or milk

2 packed cups (100 g) cubed gluten-free bread, partially dried in the oven (such as Udi's brand)

1 cup (120 g) shredded cheddar or Colby cheese

1 cup (35 g) chopped fresh spinach

1 teaspoon kosher or fine sea salt

½ teaspoon freshly ground black pepper

1 teaspoon dried thyme

¼ teaspoon garlic powder (*not* garlic salt)

1½ cups (355 ml) water for the bottom of the pot

1 Press Sauté and heat the inner pot of your electric pressure cooker. Add the oil and, when hot, add the sausage, onions, and peppers, stirring to break up clumps, until cooked through, about 5 minutes. Transfer to a large bowl and set aside to cool. Press Cancel. Wipe out the pot.

2 Butter a 7 x 3-inch (18 x 7.6 cm) round baking pan and line with parchment. Place a strip of parchment around the inside edge of the pan. Lay out a square of foil large enough to cover the pan. Set a trivet in the bottom of the inner pot and pour in 1½ cups (355 ml) water.

3 In a bowl, whisk the eggs with the half-and-half until smooth. Pour into the sausage mixture and add the bread cubes, cheese, and spinach. Season with salt and pepper,

add the thyme and garlic powder, and mix. Pour into the prepared pan, cover with the foil and crimp it closed. Use a foil sling (see page 18) to lower the pan onto the trivet.

4 Close and lock the lid, making sure the steam release handle is in the sealing position. Cook on high pressure for 17 minutes. When finished, release the pressure naturally for 12 minutes, then turn the steam release handle to venting, releasing any remaining steam. When the valve drops, unlock the lid and open it carefully.

5 Lift the pan out of the pot and set it on a wire cooling rack. Use a paper towel to blot any excess liquid on the top. Carefully remove the foil. Cut into quarters, scoop onto plates and serve immediately.

Maple-Kissed Millet Porridge

GLUTEN FREE • DAIRY-FREE OPTION • VEGETARIAN • VEGAN OPTION • SOY FREE • NUT FREE • EGG FREE

Millet is a lovely and delicious gluten-free ancient grain. A cross between oatmeal and cream of wheat, millet is a terrific way to load up on fiber and nutrients before heading out the door. The spicy aromas will remind you a little of pumpkin pie, but less so when you taste it, especially with the maple syrup sweetener. You will love this new way to kick off your day.

Yield 2 to 4 servings

1 cup (175 g) uncooked millet, rinsed well and drained

1 cup (235 ml) milk or dairy-free milk, plus extra for serving

2 cups (475 ml) water

2 tablespoons (30 ml) maple syrup, plus extra for serving

1 tablespoon (15 ml) gluten-free vanilla extract

½ teaspoon ground cinnamon

¼ teaspoon ground ginger

⅛ teaspoon ground allspice

¼ teaspoon kosher or fine sea salt

Fresh berries, for serving (optional)

1 Add all the ingredients to the inner pot of your electric pressure cooker, stirring until evenly blended. Close and lock the lid, making sure the steam release handle is in the sealing position. Cook on high pressure for 10 minutes.

2 When it is finished, release the pressure naturally for 13 minutes. Then turn the steam release handle to venting, releasing any remaining steam. Unlock the lid and open it carefully. Stir well to thoroughly distribute the spices (they tend to stay on the top layer and around the edges). Using a spatula to cut the spices into the millet works well.

3 Taste and adjust the seasonings if needed. Scoop into bowls, add a splash of milk or dairy-free milk, and top with fresh berries if desired. Pass additional maple syrup at the table.

Sweet Potato and Egg Caribbean Breakfast Burritos

GLUTEN FREE • DAIRY-FREE OPTION • SOY FREE • NUT FREE

Easy and quick breakfast options are always popular, and these Caribbean-influenced burritos are no exception. Filled with chunks of sweet potatoes, black beans, scrambled eggs, and salsa, they are a satisfying start to a busy day.

Yield 4 servings

For the potatoes

1 cup (235 ml) water or vegetable stock (page 214) for the bottom of the pot

½ pound (227 g) sweet potatoes, peeled and cut into small cubes

Kosher or fine sea salt and freshly ground black pepper

For the filling

2 tablespoons (30 ml) olive or vegetable oil, divided

½ onion, finely chopped

½ red bell pepper, seeded and finely chopped

1 teaspoon chipotle powder

1 cup (240 g) canned gluten-free black beans, rinsed and drained

6 large eggs

For assembly

4 large gluten-free tortillas, such as Mission gluten-free brand, warmed (See Note)

½ cup (120 g) gluten-free salsa, such as tomatillo, salsa verde, salsa roja, or pico de gallo

1 cup (120 g) shredded Monterey Jack, pepper Jack, or Colby cheese, optional

Freshly squeezed lime juice

Fresh cilantro leaves, chopped

(continued)

Note: To make this a low-carb meal, turn this into a burrito bowl by leaving off the tortilla. Scoop the filling into bowls and eat with a fork.

Notes: Warm the tortillas in a dry skillet or the microwave to make them pliable. If they are cold, they will crack when you try to fill and roll them. Be aware, gluten-free tortillas can be quite delicate. It is safest to eat these over a plate to catch anything that may fall out.

For a dairy-free option, leave out the cheese or use a dairy-free cheese.

Potatoes

1 Pour the water into the bottom of the inner pot of your electric pressure cooker. Place a steamer basket in the pot and pile the potatoes in the basket. Close and lock the lid, making sure the steam release handle is in the sealing position. Cook on high pressure for 2 minutes. Naturally release the pressure for 2 minutes, then quickly release the remaining pressure by turning the steam release handle to venting. Press Cancel.

2 Unlock the lid and open it carefully. Lift the potatoes out of the pot, season with salt and pepper, set aside, and keep warm. The potatoes can be cooked a day ahead and rewarmed before cooking the eggs and assembling the burritos.

Filling

1 While the potatoes are cooking, in a 10-inch (25 cm) skillet, heat 1 tablespoon (15 ml) of the oil and cook the onion and pepper for 5 minutes to soften slightly. Add the chipotle powder and beans to the skillet, heating through. Use a slotted spoon to transfer the vegetables to a bowl and cover to keep warm.

2 Add the remaining 1 tablespoon (15 ml) oil to the skillet. Beat the eggs in a bowl until blended, then pour into the skillet and cook, stirring constantly, until scrambled. Remove the pan from the heat. Using a spatula, chop the eggs into small pieces. Stir the beans and vegetables into the eggs and keep warm.

Assembly

1 Lightly warm the tortillas (see Note) and layer one-fourth of the potatoes and one-fourth of the eggs on each one. Top with 2 tablespoons (30 g) of the salsa and about ¼ cup (30 g) of the shredded cheese. Sprinkle with some lime juice and a little cilantro, carefully roll up, and serve while warm. If they are delicate and tending to tear, eat them with a fork.

Breakfast O'Brien Cottage Fries

GLUTEN FREE • DAIRY FREE •
VEGETARIAN • VEGAN • SOY FREE
• NUT FREE • EGG FREE

A wonderful addition to your breakfasts are chunky potatoes. The secret is to partially cook them first to get the creamy center and then fry for the crispy exterior. Adding onions and peppers boosts the flavor and lets you create a home-made version of the frozen variety. This is a delicious side to add to your morning meals, or for parties, brunches, or family gatherings.

Yield 4 servings

1½ pounds (680 g) Yukon Gold or Red Bliss potatoes, unpeeled

3 tablespoons (45 ml) olive oil, divided

½ onion, finely chopped

1 to 2 red bell peppers, seeded and finely chopped

2 to 3 tablespoons (20 to 30 g) gluten-free chopped green chiles (optional)

Kosher or fine sea salt and freshly ground black pepper

2 tablespoons (6 g) minced fresh parsley, for garnish

1 cup (235 ml) water for the bottom of the pot

1 Cut the potatoes into bite-size chunks. Keeping the pieces similarly sized helps everything cook at the same rate.

2 Place 1 cup (235 ml) water in the bottom of the inner pot of your electric pressure cooker. Set the trivet in the bottom and then insert a steamer basket. Place the potatoes in the basket. Close and lock the lid, making sure the steam release handle is in the sealing position. Cook on high pressure for 4 minutes.

3 When it is finished, do a quick release. Turn the steam release handle to venting, releasing any remaining steam. When the pin drops, unlock the lid and open it carefully. Press Cancel. Strain the potatoes.

4 Heat 2 tablespoons (30 ml) of the oil in a large skillet or griddle over medium-high heat. Add the onions, peppers, and chiles (if using) and cook until the onions are softened, about 3 minutes, stirring often. Move the vegetables to a bowl. Add the potatoes to the pan and add the remaining 1 tablespoon (15 ml) olive oil.

5 Cook without stirring for about 2 minutes, or until golden brown. Flip and cook the second side until browned. Stir in the vegetables to rewarm, season generously with the salt and pepper, and serve sprinkled with the parsley.

Having a flat 12-inch (30.5 cm) skillet or griddle is perfect for this recipe. It gives you room to spread the potatoes out so they can crisp easily. The trick is to leave them undisturbed until they are perfectly golden brown!

2
APPEALING APPETIZERS

Every great party starts with great food! You don't have to give up on nibbles and tidbits because of dietary restrictions. With your pressure cooker it's easy to create tantalizing dips and more substantial individual bite-size treats. Skip the store-bought versions of these classic appetizers in favor of your own gluten-free alternatives. We promise not to tell if you have more than one serving!

For a crowd, we suggest the Cherry Chipotle Chicken Wings (page 48) or a big batch of Hummus (page 46) with plenty of vegetables for dipping. On game days, you can never go wrong with Teriyaki Meatballs (page 53) or Nachos with Spicy Cheese Sauce (page 57)!

Whether you're celebrating with friends, hanging out to watch the game, or hosting a family gathering, these fast and friendly, crowd-pleasing appetizers allow you to celebrate without having to worry about watching the stove or what may be hiding in the ingredients list.

Recipes

Hummus

GLUTEN FREE • DAIRY FREE • VEGETARIAN

An added bonus of cooking beans in a pressure cooker means you don't have to soak them. With a little bit of extra time, they cook up perfectly. Make this deliciously easy hummus while the chickpeas are still warm and you'll have a smooth, light dip to serve with vegetables or gluten-free crackers.

Yield 2 cups (480 g)

1 cup (240 g) dried chickpeas

3 cups (705 ml) water

1 teaspoon salt

3 tablespoons (45 ml) olive oil, plus more for serving

¼ cup (60 g) tahini

3 tablespoons (45 ml) lemon juice

4 cloves garlic, chopped roughly

1 teaspoon ground cumin

Salt and pepper to taste

Smoked paprika, for serving

Chopped fresh parsley, for serving

1 Add the dried chickpeas to the inner pot of your electric pressure cooker. Add the water and salt.

2 Close and lock the lid, making sure the steam release knob is in the sealing position. Cook on high pressure for 60 minutes. When the cook time is finished, allow a complete natural release. When the float pin drops, unlock the lid and open it carefully.

3 Ladle 1 cup (235 ml) of the cooking liquid out of the pot and set it aside. Using mitts or a dish towel, carefully lift the inner pot out and drain the chickpeas into a colander.

4 Transfer the warm, drained chickpeas to a food processor or blender. Add the olive oil, tahini, lemon juice, garlic, cumin, and salt. Process at medium speed, slowly adding in the reserved cooking liquid. Continue until the mixture is smooth and creamy. If needed, stop and scrape down the sides of the bowl and process again to achieve the desired texture. You might not use all of the cooking liquid.

5 Taste the hummus. Adjust the seasoning with salt and pepper, if needed.

6 Serve with a drizzle of olive oil and a sprinkle of smoked paprika and parsley. Store in an air-tight container for up to 6 days.

Hot Crab Dip

GLUTEN FREE • NUT FREE

Get all the traditional flavors of a takeout crab Rangoon in a hot dip you make right in your pressure cooker. Use our homemade yogurt (page 30) for the yogurt in this recipe and take advantage of our gluten-free friend, coconut aminos, in place of soy sauce to achieve the same great flavor without the gluten.

Yield 6 servings

─────

This dip comes together much easier if all your ingredients are at room temperature.

8 ounces (227 g) cream cheese, at room temperature

⅓ cup (80 g) mayonnaise, at room temperature

⅓ cup (80 g) sour cream or plain Greek yogurt, at room temperature

16 ounces (454 g) lump crabmeat

1½ cups (180 g) shredded white cheddar cheese, divided

⅓ cup (35 g) freshly grated Parmesan cheese

4 scallions, thinly sliced

2 teaspoons (10 ml) Worcestershire sauce (Lea & Perrins is gluten free)

1 teaspoon coconut aminos (or gluten-free soy sauce)

1 teaspoon sesame oil

1 teaspoon Sriracha

2 teaspoons (7 g) minced garlic

Kosher salt and freshly ground black pepper, to taste

2 cups (470 ml) water for the bottom of the pot

1 In a large bowl, or the bowl of your stand mixer, combine all the ingredients. Mix well until thoroughly incorporated.

2 Spoon the mixture into a lightly greased 7 x 3-inch (18 x 7.6 cm) cake pan, or a pan that will fit in your pressure cooker. Cover the pan tightly with foil, crimping the edges to seal.

3 Place a trivet at the bottom of the inner pot of your pressure cooker and add 2 cups (470 ml) water.

4 Using a foil sling (see page 18), carefully lower the casserole dish into the pressure cooker. Fold the foil strips down so that they do not interfere with closing the lid.

5 Close and lock the lid, making sure the steam release handle is in the sealing position. Cook on high pressure for 10 minutes. When the cook time is finished, use a quick release by opening the release knob and venting all the steam. When the float pin drops, unlock the lid and open it carefully.

6 Remove the foil-covered dish with the sling and check the dip to make sure the cheese is completely melted. If it's not, return the lid to the pressure cooker and cook on high pressure for an additional 2 minutes, doing a quick release when the time is up. Stir to combine.

7 If you like a crispy top, slide the dish under the broiler for 1 to 2 minutes, until the top is a golden brown color.

8 Serve warm with gluten-free crackers.

Cherry Chipotle Chicken Wings

GLUTEN FREE • DAIRY FREE • NUT FREE • SOY FREE • PALEO

This will quickly become your favorite party appetizer! The chicken wings get a little crispy when you sauté them, but then are steamed to tender perfection in your pressure cooker. The sauce has a sweet and spicy kick your whole family will enjoy. There are just a few ingredients in this recipe, so you can make it any time unexpected guests pop in! If you can't find Not Ketchup, simply substitute your favorite gluten-free BBQ sauce (such as Stubb's brand).

Yield 6 servings

You can buy Not Ketchup sauces online in a variety of different flavors, including a Spiced Fig and a Tangerine Hatch Chile that would also work well with this recipe. Check out their regular Fruitchup, Smoky Date, and Blueberry White Pepper, too! They are all gluten free, dairy free, and soy free!

¼ cup (56 g) butter

1 cup (240 g) Not Ketchup Cherry Chipotle Sauce (or your favorite gluten-free BBQ/hot wing sauce)

1 tablespoon (15 ml) vegetable oil

3 to 4 pounds (1362 to 1816 g) chicken wings

Salt and pepper to taste

1 cup (235 ml) chicken stock (page 213)

Gluten-free ranch dressing, for serving

Carrot and celery sticks, for serving

1 In a small saucepan, melt the butter over low heat, then add the chipotle sauce. Cook over low heat, whisking continuously to combine. Simmer gently for 6 to 8 minutes, or until the sauce begins to thicken. Set aside.

2 Press Sauté on your electric pressure cooker. When the inner pot is hot, add the oil. Place the chicken wings in the pot and season with salt and pepper. Brown them for 5 minutes on each side. Remove to a serving plate.

3 Pour the chicken stock into the inner pot. Use a wooden spoon to gently scrape up any browned bits from the bottom of the pan.

4 Place a trivet in the bottom of the cooking pot over the stock. Place the browned wings on the trivet, being careful not to let the wings touch the stock.

5 Close and lock the lid, making sure the steam release knob is in the sealing position. Cook on high pressure for 5 minutes. When the cook time is finished, allow a 5-minute natural release, then do a quick release to vent any remaining steam. When the float pin drops, unlock the lid and open it carefully.

6 Line a baking sheet with aluminum foil. Remove the chicken wings from the pressure cooker and place on the lined baking sheet. If you have a rack that fits in the baking sheet, even better! The air circulating around the wings as they sit on the rack will make your wings extra crispy. If you don't have a rack, just put the wings on the foil-lined baking sheet. They will still get crispy.

7 Generously brush the wings with the warm sauce and broil for 7 minutes on each side. If they are not crispy enough, broil for 2 to 3 minutes more on each side.

8 Remove from the oven and, if desired, toss the wings quickly in the remaining sauce. Serve with gluten-free ranch dressing alongside some carrot and celery sticks.

Spinach Artichoke Dip

GLUTEN FREE • SOY FREE • NUT FREE
• VEGETARIAN

A must-have game-day appetizer, this dip will easily feed a crowd. This time-honored, highly addictive dip is a blend of cheesy good-ness that uses ingredients you probably have in your pantry. We love that you put everything together in your mixer and then cook it in the pressure cooker. This dip goes together as quickly as it will disappear and makes a great quick snack for a stay-at-home movie night, too!

Yield 10 servings

1 (10-ounce, or 280 g) package frozen spinach, thawed, chopped, and well drained

1 (14-ounce, or 392 g) can artichoke hearts, drained and coarsely chopped

4 cloves garlic, minced

½ cup (80 g) finely chopped onion

1 (8-ounce, or 227 g) block cream cheese, softened to room temperature and cut into cubes

1 cup (100 g) grated Parmesan cheese

1 cup (120 g) shredded mozzarella cheese

½ cup (120 g) sour cream or plain Greek yogurt

½ teaspoon salt

¾ teaspoon freshly ground black pepper

⅛ teaspoon cayenne pepper

2 cups (470 ml) water for the bottom of the pot

Gluten-free crackers, for serving

1 In a large bowl, or the bowl of your stand mixer, combine the spinach, artichokes, garlic, onion, cream cheese, Parme-san, mozzarella, sour cream, and seasonings. Mix well until thoroughly incorporated.

2 Spoon the mixture into a lightly greased 1½ quart (1.4 L) baking dish or a 7 x 3-inch (18 x 7.6 cm) cake pan that will fit in your pressure cooker. Cover the baking dish tightly with foil.

3 Place a trivet at the bottom of the inner pot of your pres-sure cooker and add the 2 cups (470 ml) water.

4 Using a foil sling (see page 18), carefully lower the cas-serole dish into the pressure cooker. Fold the foil strips down so that they do not interfere with closing the lid.

5 Close and lock the lid, making sure the steam release knob is in the sealing position. Cook on high pressure for 10 minutes. When the cook time is finished, use a quick release by opening the release knob and venting all the steam. When the float pin drops, unlock the lid and open it carefully.

6 Remove the foil-covered dish with the sling and check the dip to make sure the cheese is completely melted. Stir to combine. If you like a crispy top, slide the casserole dish under the broiler for 2 minutes until the cheese is a golden brown color. Watch carefully so it doesn't burn.

7 Serve warm with gluten-free crackers.

Delightfully Delicious Deviled Eggs

GLUTEN FREE • DAIRY FREE • SOY FREE • NUT FREE • VEGETARIAN • PALEO

One of the most wonderful things about an electric pressure cooker is the ability to cook hard-boiled eggs. Steaming the eggs under pressure creates the best, easy-to-peel eggs you've ever had. If you have ever lost half the egg white because the peel stuck, this method will make you love making them again. This classic variation of traditional deviled eggs adds hot sauce for a spicy kick!

Yield 24 servings

For the hard-boiled eggs

1 cup (235 ml) cold water

12 large eggs, straight from the refrigerator

Large bowl of water with ice

For the deviled eggs

12 hard-boiled eggs

⅔ cup (160 g) mayonnaise

1 tablespoon (6 g) dry mustard powder

2 teaspoons (10 ml) hot sauce

Salt and pepper to taste

Smoked paprika, for garnish

Scallions, sliced on the diagonal, green parts only, for garnish

Hard-boiled eggs

1 Pour the cold water in the inner cooking pot. Place a steam rack or trivet in the inner pot of your pressure cooker. Place the eggs on the trivet.

2 Close and lock the lid, making sure the steam release knob is in the sealing position. Cook on high pressure for 6 minutes (depending on how soft or firm you like the yolk). Naturally release the pressure for 6 minutes, then unlock the lid and open it carefully. Turn off the machine.

3 Remove the eggs and immediately plunge them into the bowl of ice water to stop the cooking. Let them sit for 6 to 10 minutes. If serving immediately, peel the eggs under running water. Store unpeeled eggs in the refrigerator up to 1 week.

Deviled eggs

1 Peel the hard-boiled eggs and slice in half. Remove the yolks and set aside.

2 In the bowl of a food processor, pulse hard egg yolks until they resemble yellow sand. Add the mayonnaise, mustard, and hot sauce. Blend until the mixture is smooth and creamy. If you don't have a food processor, combine the ingredients in a medium bowl and use a hand mixer to get the desired consistency. Add salt and pepper to taste.

3 Fill the hollows of the egg whites with the yolk mix. Sprinkle with smoked paprika and scallions to garnish.

Steamed Artichokes with Spicy Garlic Aioli

GLUTEN FREE • NUT FREE • SOY FREE • VEGETARIAN

Artichokes are full of fiber and high in antioxidants, plus they taste great! There is a tiny restaurant on the beach in Moss Landing, California, that serves fresh steamed artichokes from a nearby farm to local beach-goers. Eating them, dipped in a spicy garlic aioli, while enjoying the sun and sand is a decadent treat. The aioli has just enough garlic to give it a pleasant zing, but feel free to add more if you are a garlic lover! This recipe can be used as an appetizer to feed several people or can be made into a special meal for two.

Yield 6 servings

If the spicy garlic dip isn't for you, make a simple dip with melted butter, a bit of dill, and some grated Parmesan cheese.

For the artichokes

3 medium artichokes
1 whole lemon, cut into quarters
1 cup (235 ml) water
¼ cup (60 ml) lemon juice
3 cloves garlic, smashed

For the spicy garlic aioli

3 tablespoons (45 g) plain Greek yogurt
2 tablespoons (30 g) mayonnaise
4 cloves garlic, minced
½ teaspoon cayenne pepper
¼ teaspoon garlic powder
½ teaspoon coarsely ground black pepper
Pinch of salt

Artichokes

1 Use a serrated knife to cut the top third off each artichoke. Cut the stems off at the base. Rinse the artichokes well. Rub one of the lemon quarters all over the cut tops of the artichoke to prevent them from browning.

2 Add the lemon quarters, water, lemon juice, and garlic to the pot. Place a steam rack or trivet in the inner pot of your pressure cooker. Place the artichokes on the trivet.

3 Close and lock the lid, making sure the steam release knob is in the sealing position. Cook on high pressure for 12 minutes. When the cook time is finished, use a quick release method. Move the release knob to the venting position and vent all the steam. When all the steam has been expelled and the float pin drops, unlock the lid and open it carefully.

4 Pull off an artichoke leaf to test for doneness; it should come off without any resistance. Carefully lift the artichokes from the inner pot of your pressure cooker with a pair of tongs. Set aside to cool while you make the aioli.

Aioli

1 In a medium bowl, combine all the ingredients for the aioli and whisk until smooth.

2 Serve the artichokes on a plate with the aioli.

Teriyaki Meatballs

GLUTEN FREE • NUT FREE

These tender, juicy meatballs come together quickly and get cooked in an easy home-made teriyaki sauce. We use ground turkey in place of traditional ground beef and swap out gluten-filled soy sauce with coconut aminos for a gluten-free alternative. The cornstarch slurry turns the sauce into a rich glaze for the meatballs. All you need to do is put them on a plate and serve them to your guests.

Yield 40 meatballs

For the teriyaki sauce

1 cup (235 ml) coconut aminos or gluten-free soy sauce

½ cup (120 ml) rice wine vinegar

4 cloves garlic, minced

1 tablespoon (8 g) freshly grated ginger

2 tablespoons (30 ml) vegetable oil

2 teaspoons (10 ml) sesame oil

⅓ cup (75 g) brown sugar

2 tablespoons (40 g) honey

1 teaspoon black pepper

For the meatballs

2 pounds (908 g) ground turkey meat (Jennie-O is gluten free)

½ cup (60 g) gluten-free panko bread crumbs

2 large eggs

½ cup (50 g) thinly sliced scallion, green parts only, divided

1 teaspoon garlic powder

1 teaspoon salt

1½ teaspoons freshly cracked black pepper

2 tablespoons (30 ml) vegetable oil

2 tablespoons (16 g) cornstarch

2 tablespoons (30 ml) cold water

1 tablespoon (8 g) sesame seeds, for garnish

Teriyaki Sauce

1 Combine the coconut aminos, vinegar, garlic, ginger, vegetable oil, sesame oil, brown sugar, honey, and pepper in a medium bowl. Set aside.

Meatballs

1 In a large bowl, combine the ground turkey, bread crumbs, eggs, ¼ cup (25 g) of the scallions, garlic powder, salt, and pepper. Using a scant 1 ounce (28 g), gently shape into 40 meatballs.

2 Press Sauté on your electric pressure cooker. When the inner pot is hot, add the oil. When the oil is hot, add enough meatballs to cover the bottom of the pot, browning for about 2 minutes per side. Remove to a serving platter while you brown the rest.

(continued)

For a meal, serve meatballs over white rice with extra sauce!

3 When all the meatballs are browned, return them to the pot and pour the teriyaki sauce over them.

4 Close and lock the lid, making sure the steam release handle is in the sealing position. Cook on high pressure for 15 minutes. When the cook time is finished, allow a natural release for 10 minutes, then do a quick release to vent any remaining steam. Once the float pin drops, you can safely unlock the lid. Press Cancel.

5 In a small bowl, whisk together the cornstarch and water until it forms a slurry. Press Sauté and when the mixture starts to bubble, add the slurry to the pot, continuing to stir until the sauce thickens considerably around the meatballs, 3 to 5 minutes.

6 To serve, transfer the meatballs to a large platter. Skewer each one with a decorative toothpick and sprinkle with the remaining ¼ cup (25 g) sliced scallions and the sesame seeds.

Eggplant and Olive Spread

GLUTEN FREE • VEGETARIAN
• DAIRY FREE

This eggplant dip is a variation of baba ganoush. It is rich, creamy, and blended to the perfect dippable consistency. Traditionally, the vegetables are grilled for baba ganoush, but in this case, use the highest setting of Sauté or Browning on your pressure cooker to give the onions and eggplant a good char. It may take a little while, but you'll love the smoky flavor it adds to your dip.

Yield 6 servings

Add a teaspoon of chili powder to the recipe if you like your dip on the spicy side.

2 tablespoons (30 ml) olive oil

1 small brown onion, peeled and cut in half

2 pounds (908 g) eggplant, peeled and cut into large chunks

5 cloves garlic

1 tablespoon (4 g) fresh oregano leaves

1 teaspoon salt

1 cup (235 ml) vegetable stock (page 214)

3 tablespoons (30 ml) lemon juice

1½ tablespoons (23 g) tahini

Salt and pepper, to taste

½ cup (50 g) pitted black olives (reserve a few for garnish)

1 tablespoon (2 g) chiffonade fresh Thai basil leaves, for garnish

¼ cup (40 g) diced cherry tomatoes, for garnish

Extra virgin olive oil, for drizzling

Gluten-free crackers or celery sticks, for serving

1 Press Sauté on your electric pressure cooker. Adjust, if possible, to the highest setting. When the inner pot is hot, add the olive oil. When the oil has heated, carefully place the onion halves, cut side down, in the pot. Let them sear until the onions get very brown. Add the eggplant and garlic cloves. Let them get browned as well, watching carefully so the garlic cloves don't burn. Press Cancel.

2 Add the oregano, salt, and vegetable stock to the browned vegetables, stirring well.

3 Close and lock the lid, making sure the steam release handle is in the sealing position. Press Manual and cook on high pressure for 3 minutes. When the cook time is finished, do a quick pressure release by carefully moving the sealing handle to venting and allowing all the steam to escape. When the float pin drops, unlock the lid and open the lid carefully.

4 Using mini mitts or a dish towel, carefully remove the inner cooking pot from the base and strain the eggplant mixture in a large colander, reserving ¼ cup (60 ml) of the cooking liquid.

5 Place the eggplant mixture in a blender. Add the lemon juice, tahini, and olives. Blend, using some of the cooking liquid to help reach the desired consistency. You may not need all the liquid. Taste and adjust the seasoning, adding salt and pepper if needed.

6 Scrape into a serving bowl and sprinkle with the remaining whole olives, basil leaves, and tomatoes, and drizzle with the extra virgin olive oil. Serve with gluten-free crackers or celery sticks.

Nachos with Spicy Cheese Sauce

GLUTEN FREE • SOY FREE • NUT FREE

Fully loaded nachos with a spicy homemade beer-cheese sauce are a must for any get-together. If you're serving this at a party, set up a nacho bar so everyone can customize the nachos with their own favorite toppings. Options might include grilled chicken or carne asada, thinly sliced cabbage, diced red onions or scallions, sour cream, black beans, and fresh guacamole. We like the subtle heat of poblano peppers in this cheese sauce, but if you prefer a spicier sauce, swap out the poblanos for Anaheim peppers or serranos.

Yield 8 servings

Note: Be sure to use certified gluten-free tortilla chips. Some have wheat added and some are made in facilities where gluten-full products are also processed, posing a cross-contamination issue. It is always better to be careful and safe when serving those who cannot have gluten.

1 tablespoon (15 ml) vegetable oil

½ yellow onion, diced

2 poblano peppers, seeded and diced

2 teaspoons (6 g) chili powder

½ teaspoon ground cumin

½ teaspoon salt

1 (12-ounce, or 336 ml) bottle Ipswich Ale Brewery Celia Saison (or your favorite gluten-free beer)

1 (10-ounce, or 280 g) can diced tomatoes with jalapeños

12 ounces (336 g) sharp cheddar cheese, grated

12 ounces (336 g) Monterey Jack cheese, grated

3 tablespoons (24 g) cornstarch

Gluten-free corn tortilla chips, such as Mission brand, for serving (see Note)

Nacho toppings, as desired

1 Press Sauté on your electric pressure cooker. When the inner pot is hot, add the oil. When the oil is hot, add the onion and poblano. Cook for 3 to 5 minutes, or until softened.

2 Add the chili powder, cumin, and salt and cook for 1 minute, or until very fragrant. Add the beer and diced tomatoes, scraping the bottom of the pan and stirring well to combine.

3 Close and lock the lid, making sure the steam release handle is in the sealing position. Cook on high pressure for 5 minutes.

4 While the sauce is cooking, in a bowl, toss the grated cheeses with the cornstarch, mixing well to make sure each shred is coated with the cornstarch.

5 When the cook time is finished, allow a 5-minute natural release, then do a quick release to vent any remaining steam. When the float pin drops, unlock the lid and open it carefully. Press Cancel.

6 Working quickly, add the coated cheese in handfuls to the beer mixture, whisking vigorously to combine. Once all of the cheese has been incorporated, set your pressure cooker to Keep Warm (if it has one) while you prepare the rest of the nachos. You may need to stir the sauce again before serving.

7 Scatter the tortilla chips on a platter, add your favorite nacho toppings, ladle the cheese sauce over the top, and enjoy!

3

SPECTACULAR SOUPS AND STEWS

Soups and stews are some of the best and easiest foods to make in your pressure cooker. The pressure tenderizes even the hardest ingredients, like butternut squash, in a fraction of the time and beans are cooked so quickly you almost don't have time to make the garnishes.

Because there is no evaporation during cooking, there will be less liquid called for in these recipes than you are accustomed to seeing. This helps concentrate the flavors and avoids having the soups and stews become watered down. One way to intensify the flavors is to use bouillon, soup base, or demi-glace. These are highly concentrated granules and pastes

you can add by the spoonful. Most bases contain gluten, so be careful to get a gluten-free variety. Herb-Ox brand has a line of gluten-free bouillons that are quite good.

It is very important to never fill the pot above the maximum fill line on the inner pot, about two-thirds full. You need room at the top of the pot. Also, the more liquid you have in the pot, the longer it will take to come to pressure and to release—just like on the stove, it always takes longer for a large pot of water to come to a boil.

If you want to thicken your soups and stews a bit, you can always turn on Sauté, bring the mixture to a boil, and reduce the liquid with the lid off. For more thickening power, try using a starch. Because you won't be able to stir while the lid is locked, avoid using gluten-free flour during cooking, such as for dredging meats in flour and browning before cooking. The best solution is to thicken the liquid after cooking by adding a cornstarch slurry, which is cornstarch dissolved in cool water. If you cannot have corn products, use half as much potato starch (*not* potato flour) as called for in the recipe. See page 24 for more information on thickeners.

Recipes

Dreamy Creamy Tomato Soup

GLUTEN FREE • VEGETARIAN • SOY FREE • NUT FREE • EGG FREE

One bite of this soup and you will be transported back to childhood, sunny days, scraped knees, and braces. Packed with bold tomato flavor enhanced with herbs and vegetables, this soup definitely doesn't come out of a can! Don't be surprised when your family and friends beg you to make this soup over and over again.

Yield About 4 servings

When a recipe highlights an ingredient like this recipe does tomatoes, it pays to use the best you can afford. Pomi brand tomatoes are imported from Northern Italy and are consistently high quality for the best-tasting recipes. They come in boxes and can be found at many major grocery stores across the nation.

2 tablespoons (28 g) butter or (30 ml) olive oil, divided

1 medium onion, finely chopped

3 carrots, finely chopped

3 stalks celery, finely chopped

½ red bell pepper, seeded and finely chopped

1 clove garlic, minced

2 cups (470 ml) chicken stock (page 213)

About 50 ounces (1500 g) chopped or crushed tomatoes, such as Pomi brand

2 teaspoons (1 g) dried oregano

2 teaspoons (1 g) dried basil

½ teaspoon dried crushed rosemary

1 bay leaf

1 teaspoon granulated sugar

2 teaspoons (12 g) kosher or fine sea salt

1 teaspoon freshly ground black pepper

½ cup (120 ml) heavy cream or half-and-half

2 tablespoons (4 g) finely minced fresh basil leaves, plus whole leaves for garnish

1 Press Sauté and heat the inner pot of your electric pressure cooker. Melt 1 tablespoon (14 g) of the butter. Add the onion, carrots, celery, and bell pepper and cook for 3 minutes, stirring, to soften. Stir in the garlic and cook for 30 seconds. Add the stock, tomatoes, herbs, sugar, salt, and pepper. Stir to combine. Press Cancel.

2 Close and lock the lid, making sure the steam release handle is in the sealing position. Cook on high pressure for 5 minutes. When it is finished, release the pressure naturally for 10 minutes, then turn the steam release handle to venting, releasing any remaining steam. Unlock the lid and open it carefully. Press Cancel.

3 Remove and discard the bay leaf. Stir in the remaining 1 tablespoon (14 g) butter and stir until it is melted. Use an immersion blender to puree the soup in the pot. You can also use a blender, but puree in batches—hot liquids expand!

4 Stir in the cream and chopped basil. Taste and adjust the seasonings if needed. Ladle into bowls, garnish with basil leaves, and serve.

Beef "Barley" Soup with Sorghum

GLUTEN FREE • DAIRY FREE • SOY FREE • NUT FREE

One of the most-missed soups for those who can no longer have gluten ingredients is beef barley soup. It was challenging finding anything that could approximate the flavor and texture of the barley, but sorghum is extremely versatile and makes a good substitute. It can be ground into a flour that is delicious in breads and other baked goods. It can be turned into a syrup that brings back memories of simpler times. And you can use it whole, which, when cooked, becomes a tantalizingly chewy grain that is reminiscent of barley.

Yield About 4 servings

2 tablespoons (30 ml) olive or vegetable oil

1½ pounds (680 g) beef chuck roast, fat trimmed and meat cut into 1-inch (2.5 cm) cubes

1 large onion, chopped

2 cloves garlic, minced

2 carrots, trimmed and chopped

2 stalks celery, trimmed and chopped

1 tablespoon (15 g) tomato paste

1 teaspoon minced fresh rosemary leaves

1 teaspoon fresh thyme leaves

6½ cups (1528 ml) beef stock (page 212) or gluten-free store-bought stock (see Note)

1 cup (200 g) whole-grain sorghum, rinsed and drained

2 bay leaves

Kosher or fine sea salt and ground black pepper, to taste

1 Press Sauté and pour the oil into the inner pot of your electric pressure cooker. Brown the beef on all sides, working in batches so you can leave room between the pieces as they cook. Transfer the browned beef to a plate; set aside.

2 Add the onion and garlic to the oil in the pot. Cook, stirring often, until the onion has begun to soften, about 3 minutes. Stir in the carrots, celery, tomato paste, rosemary, and thyme. Cook for another 3 minutes, stirring regularly. Pour in the stock and scrape the bottom of the pot to release any browned bits. Add the sorghum and bay leaves. Return the beef to the pot. Press Cancel.

3 Close and lock the lid, making sure the steam release handle is in the sealing position. Cook on high pressure for 40 minutes. When it is finished, release the pressure naturally for 10 minutes, then turn the steam release handle to venting, releasing remaining steam. Unlock the lid and carefully open.

4 Taste the stock and adjust the seasoning with salt and pepper as desired. Remove and discard the bay leaves. Ladle into bowls and serve.

Whole-grain sorghum can be challenging to find. If it isn't readily available in your local grocery store, you can order it online from Bob's Red Mill (www.bobsredmill.com).

Note: Using homemade stock lets you control the amount of salt in your dishes. If you use canned beef stock, it will likely be saltier than homemade. If you taste the soup and it is too salty, you can add more water to dilute it.

Rib-Stickin' Chili

GLUTEN FREE • DAIRY-FREE OPTION
• SOY FREE • NUT FREE • EGG FREE

This is one of the easiest recipes to make in your electric pressure cooker and it's a real crowd-pleaser. Sauté the meats and veggies, put everything in the pot, and cook it. There is no stirring or babysitting required, and you get bold, long-cooked flavor in under an hour!

Yield 4 to 6 servings

2 tablespoons (30 ml) olive or vegetable oil

1 pound (454 g) lean ground beef

1 pound (454 g) bulk gluten-free ground sausage or Homemade Sausage (page 35)

1 large onion, diced

3 carrots, trimmed and diced

2 poblano peppers, seeded and diced

1 bell pepper, cored, seeded, and diced

2 jalapeño peppers, seeded and minced (see Note)

1 (28-ounce, or 794 g) can diced tomatoes with their juice

½ cup (120 ml) beef stock (page 212) or water

1 tablespoon (15 ml) Worcestershire sauce (Lea & Perrins brand is gluten free)

¼ cup (32 g) chili powder (Penzeys brand is gluten free)

1 tablespoon (3 g) dried oregano

2 teaspoons (4 g) smoked paprika

1 teaspoon chipotle powder (or to taste)

1 teaspoon garlic powder

1 teaspoon ground cumin

2 teaspoons (12 g) kosher or fine sea salt

1 teaspoon freshly ground black pepper

2 tablespoons (16 g) masa harina or corn flour (Bob's Red Mill brand is gluten free)

¼ cup (60 ml) cool water

Optional toppings and accompaniments

Gluten-free corn tortillas, such as Mission brand (see sidebar, page 42)

Sliced jalapeño peppers

Shredded cheddar cheese or dairy-free cheese

Minced red onion

Lime wedges

Sour cream or dairy-free sour cream

Chopped fresh parsley or cilantro

Traditional Texas chili has no beans in it, and this version doesn't either. For those who love beans in their chili, you can add gluten-free canned black beans, kidney beans, or pinto beans that have been rinsed and drained. Two (15-ounce, 428 g) cans will be filling and delicious. Stir them in at the end when you add the masa harina so they have time to warm up.

1 Press Sauté on your electric pressure cooker and heat for 30 seconds. Add the oil and the meats and cook, stirring to break up clumps, until no pink is visible. Stir in the onion, carrots, poblanos, bell pepper, and jalapeños. Cook, stirring, for 3 more minutes. Stir in the tomatoes, stock, Worcestershire, and seasonings, scraping the bottom of the pot to release any browned bits. Press Cancel.

2 Close and lock the lid, making sure the steam release handle is in the sealing position. Cook on high pressure for 30 minutes. When it is finished, release the pressure naturally for 12 minutes, then turn the handle to venting and release the remaining pressure. Unlock the lid and open it carefully. Press Cancel.

3 Press Sauté. Dissolve the masa harina in the water, whisk it into the chili, and cook, stirring often, for 3 to 5 minutes, or until the chili thickens to the consistency you like. Taste and adjust the seasonings. Press Cancel.

4 Ladle into bowls and serve with gluten-free corn tortillas and your favorite toppings.

Note: If you like spicy foods, you can add chopped serrano or habanero peppers or more chipotle powder to the chili. Remember that seasonings get stronger as they rest, so start with a lighter hand and increase the amounts slowly.

Vegan Wild Rice Soup with Cashew Cream

GLUTEN FREE • DAIRY FREE • VEGETARIAN • VEGAN • SOY FREE • EGG FREE

This soup is so good that even non-vegans will enjoy it and never miss the meat and dairy! The wild rice and chickpeas are very filling and the cashew cream adds a lovely lushness. Using homemade vegetable stock (page 214) lets you control the flavor profile and the quality of the ingredients. This soup is perfect for lunch or as the starter for a bigger meal.

Yield About 6 servings

For the soup

2 tablespoons (30 ml) olive or vegetable oil

1½ cups (240 g) diced onion

3 cloves garlic, minced

1 cup (130 g) diced carrot

1 cup (120 g) diced celery

1 cup (230 g) organic dried chickpeas, soaked for 4 hours or overnight and drained

1¼ cups (200 g) organic wild rice or a wild rice blend

1 bay leaf

1 tablespoon (2 g) fresh thyme leaves

5 cups (1175 ml) vegetable stock (page 214) or water

Kosher or fine sea salt and freshly ground black pepper, to taste

For the cashew cream (optional)

½ cup (55 g) raw cashews, soaked for 30 minutes in hot water and then drained

½ cup (120 ml) fresh water

Soup

1 Press Sauté on your electric pressure cooker. Add the oil to the inner pot and when it is hot, add the onions. Cook the onions until softened and translucent, about 4 minutes. Add the garlic and cook for 30 seconds, until fragrant. Stir in the carrots and celery. Cook until the vegetables are softened, about 4 minutes.

2 Add the drained chickpeas, wild rice, bay leaf, thyme, and stock. Stir well. Close and lock the lid, making sure the steam release handle is in the sealing position. Cook on high pressure for 25 minutes.

Cashew Cream

1 While the soup is cooking, make the cashew cream. Blend the soaked and drained cashews with the ½ cup (120 ml) fresh water in a blender until completely smooth. Set aside.

2 When the soup is finished, release the pressure naturally. Turn the steam release handle to venting, releasing any remaining steam. When the float pin drops, unlock the lid and open it carefully. Stir in the cashew cream (if using) until completely incorporated. Add salt and pepper to taste. Serve immediately.

Pasta e Fagioli (Italian Bean and Pasta Soup)

GLUTEN FREE • DAIRY-FREE OPTION • VEGETARIAN OPTION • SOY FREE • NUT FREE • EGG FREE

Sometimes called pasta fazool, pasta e fagioli is a classic Italian peasant dish served throughout Italy all year long. Loaded with pasta, beans, and sausage, it is a meal in a bowl and a great way to feed a crowd for very little money. If you want to make a vegetarian version, leave out the meat and use vegetable stock—it will be just as delicious!

Yield 6 to 8 servings

For the pasta

6 ounces (168 g) elbow pasta, such as Barilla gluten-free brand

2 teaspoons (12 g) kosher or fine sea salt

Olive or vegetable oil

For the soup

2 tablespoons (30 ml) olive oil

1 medium onion, finely chopped

1 carrot, finely chopped

1 stalk celery, finely chopped

1 pound (454 g) gluten-free ground turkey or ground pork

1 teaspoon thyme leaves

1 teaspoon dried oregano

1 teaspoon chili powder (McCormick and Penzeys brands have gluten-free versions)

½ teaspoon dried ground rosemary

½ teaspoon kosher or fine sea salt

¼ teaspoon freshly ground black pepper

3 cloves garlic, chopped

¼ cup (60 ml) gluten-free dry white wine or water (see Note, page 133)

2 cups (470 g) tomato sauce or crushed tomatoes

1 quart (940 ml) chicken stock (page 213) or vegetable stock (page 214)

2 bay leaves

1 (15-ounce, or 420 g) can gluten-free cannellini beans, rinsed and drained

Grated Parmigiano-Reggiano or Romano cheese or your favorite dairy-free cheese, for serving

Roughly chopped fresh basil leaves, for serving

Pasta

1 Place the pasta in the inner pot of your electric pressure cooker, cover with water, and sprinkle with the salt. Stir to make sure nothing is sticking to the bottom of the pot. Close and lock the lid, making sure the steam release handle is in the sealing position. Cook on high pressure for 1 minute, release the pressure naturally for 4 minutes, then do a controlled release by holding the handle halfway between the open and closed positions. Protect your hand with an oven hot pad. When all the steam has been released, press Cancel.

2 When the float pin drops, unlock the lid and open it carefully. Pour the pasta into a colander and drain. Rinse with cool water to stop the cooking. Drizzle with a little oil and toss to keep the pasta from sticking together as it sits. Set aside and stir occasionally.

Soup

1 Press Sauté and heat the oil in the inner pot of your electric pressure cooker. Add the onion, carrot, and celery, cooking until softened, about 4 minutes, stirring occasionally. Add the meat and cook until browned, using a flat spatula to break up clumps. Season with the thyme, oregano, chili powder, rosemary, salt, and pepper. When the meat is cooked through, stir in the garlic and cook for an additional 30 seconds, until fragrant. Pour in the wine and deglaze the pot, scraping up any browned bits off the bottom.

2 Stir in the tomato sauce and stock, then add the bay leaves and drained beans. Close and lock the lid, making sure the steam release handle is in the sealing position. Cook on high pressure for 3 minutes. When it is finished, release the pressure naturally for 10 minutes, then turn the steam release handle to venting, releasing any remaining steam. When the pressure valve drops, unlock the lid and open it carefully. Press Cancel.

3 Stir the cooked pasta into the pot, replace the lid, and let sit for a few minutes to reheat. Taste and adjust the seasonings if needed. Ladle the soup into bowls, top with some of the cheese and basil, and serve immediately.

Note: The timing for the pasta may change depending on the brand of pasta you use. See page 98 for details.

Chile Tortilla Soup

GLUTEN FREE • DAIRY-FREE OPTION
• VEGETARIAN OPTION • SOY FREE
• NUT FREE • EGG FREE

This soup will have you dreaming of New Mexico. It is packed with the flavors of the Southwest—chiles, vegetables, and corn— infused with tomato-flavored chicken stock. Top it with spicy homemade tortilla strips for a delightful crunch in every bite.

Yield 4 to 6 servings

For the tortilla strips

Gluten-free corn tortillas, such as Mission brand (see Note)

Olive oil, for brushing

Kosher salt and ancho chile powder

For the soup

2 tablespoons (30 ml) olive or vegetable oil

1 medium onion, finely chopped

2 carrots, trimmed and finely chopped

2 stalks celery, trimmed and finely chopped

1 tablespoon (8 g) ancho chile powder or gluten-free chili powder (McCormick and Penzeys have many gluten-free offerings), or to taste

2 teaspoons (6 g) ground cumin

1 teaspoon dried oregano

1 clove garlic, minced

1 quart (940 ml) chicken stock (page 213), divided

16 ounces (454 g) crushed or strained tomatoes

2 to 2½ pounds (908 to 1135 g) boneless, skinless chicken thighs

¼ cup (30 g) gluten-free masa harina or corn flour (Bob's Red Mill brand is gluten free)

2 cups (260 g) frozen corn kernels

For the garnishes

Fresh cilantro leaves

Avocado chunks

Shredded cheese such as pepper Jack, cheddar, or Colby

Note: Just because you find corn tortillas doesn't mean they are gluten free. Many manufacturers add it because wheat flour helps keep them pliable, making them unsafe for anyone following a gluten-free diet. Always carefully read the labels of every product you buy!

Tortilla Strips

1 Preheat the oven to 350°F (180°C, or gas mark 4). Brush the tortillas on both sides with the oil and cut into thin strips. Spread them out on a parchment-lined baking sheet, sprinkle with salt and chile powder, and bake until lightly golden brown and slightly crispy, tossing occasionally, about 15 minutes. Remove from the oven and set aside.

Soup

1 Press Sauté and heat the inner pot of your electric pressure cooker. Add the oil and, when hot, add the onions, carrots, and celery. Sprinkle with the chile powder, cumin, and oregano. Cook, stirring often, for about 4 minutes to slightly soften the vegetables. Stir in the garlic and cook for 30 seconds. Add 1 cup (235 ml) of the stock to deglaze the pan, scraping up any browned bits from the bottom of the pot. Pour in the remaining 3 cups (705 ml) stock and the tomatoes. Press Cancel.

2 Tuck the chicken into the liquids, then close and lock the lid, making sure the steam release handle is in the sealing position. Cook on high pressure for 12 minutes. When it is finished, release the pressure naturally for 15 minutes, then turn the steam release handle to venting, releasing any remaining steam. Press Cancel. Unlock the lid and open it carefully.

3 Transfer the chicken to a cutting board and chop or shred into small bite-size pieces. Press Sauté, whisk the masa harina into the soup, and bring to a boil, stirring constantly until thickened slightly. Return the chicken pieces to the pot and stir in the corn kernels. Press Cancel, place the lid on the pressure cooker, and leave to rest for 6 minutes to reheat the chicken and corn. Taste and adjust the seasonings if needed.

Serve

1 Ladle the soup into bowls and garnish with the crispy tortilla strips, cilantro, and avocado. Sprinkle cheese on top and serve immediately.

Chile Verde Pork Stew

GLUTEN FREE • DAIRY FREE • SOY FREE • NUT FREE • EGG FREE

This chile verde was inspired by a visit to Santa Fe. It was love at first sip, creating a life-long love affair with the flavors of the Southwest. Today's pressure cookers make it simple and fast to get deep, long-simmered flavor, helping you recreate this wonderful New Mexican stew in no time.

Yield 6 to 8 servings

For the homemade salsa verde

2 pounds (908 g) fresh New Mexico or poblano chiles, seeded and chopped

1 pound (454 g) fresh tomatillos, husked and rinsed well, or 1 (28-ounce, or 784 g) can whole tomatillos

1 jalapeño pepper, seeded and chopped (optional)

¼ cup (4 g) fresh cilantro leaves

½ teaspoon onion powder (*not* onion salt)

Pinch each of kosher or fine sea salt and freshly ground black pepper

For the chile verde

3 pounds (1362 g) pork shoulder or pork butt

2 tablespoons (30 ml) olive or vegetable oil, divided

2 cups (470 ml) chicken stock (page 213)

1 onion, chopped

4 cloves garlic, minced

1 tablespoon (2 g) dried oregano

2 teaspoons (6 g) ground cumin

1 teaspoon chipotle powder (optional)

1½ cups (355 g) salsa verde, homemade (see below) or store-bought

Kosher or fine sea salt and freshly ground black pepper, to taste

Steamed rice (page 82), for serving

Fresh lime wedges, for serving

Gluten-free corn tortillas, such as Mission brand, for serving (see sidebar, page 68)

Salsa Verde

1 Place the chiles and fresh husked tomatillos on a baking sheet. If using canned tomatillos, no need to cook them. Place the baking sheet under the broiler and cook for about 4 minutes, until the chiles are blistered and the tomatillos have brown spots on them. Turn everything over and broil again for about 3 minutes, or until blackened. Transfer the chiles to a bowl and cover with a clean kitchen towel. Let them steam for a few minutes. Peel the blackened skins off the chiles. Combine the chiles (with their juices), tomatillos, jalapeño, cilantro, and onion powder in a blender. Add a pinch of salt and blend until smooth. Pour into a measuring cup. Add enough water to bring this to 2 cups (470 ml) and stir to blend. Taste and adjust the seasonings if needed.

Chile Verde

1 Trim the fat from the meat and cut into 1-inch (2.5 cm) cubes. Press Sauté on your electric pressure cooker. Heat 1 tablespoon (15 ml) of the oil until shimmering in the inner pot. Add the pork in batches, browning on all sides. Use a slotted spoon to transfer the pork to a plate and continue browning the rest of the pork. When the pork is browned, place all of it back in the inner pot and add the chicken stock. Be sure to scrape the bottom of the pot to release any browned bits. Close and lock the lid, making sure the steam release handle is in the sealing position. Cook on high pressure for 20 minutes.

2 When it is finished, release the pressure naturally for 10 minutes, and then quick release the remaining steam. Unlock the lid and open it carefully. Use a slotted spoon to transfer the pork to a bowl; set aside. Press Cancel. Strain the cooking liquid through a fat separator or skim the fat from the surface and keep the remaining liquid separately.

3 Add the remaining 1 table-spoon (15 ml) oil to the pot and press Sauté. When hot, add the onion and cook, stirring, until softened, about 3 minutes. Add the garlic, oregano, cumin, and chipotle (if using) and cook just until fragrant, about 30 seconds. Add the cooked pork and stir everything together to distribute the seasonings. Pour in the salsa verde plus as much of the reserved cooking liquid as you need to reach the consistency you like. Cook for 3 minutes to blend the flavors. Taste and adjust the seasonings if needed.

4 Serve hot over cooked rice with fresh lime wedges and gluten-free corn tortillas.

For a faster option, if you can find a gluten-free salsa verde in your area, you can substitute that for the homemade version, but homemade always tastes better!

Spicy Butternut Squash Soup

GLUTEN FREE • DAIRY FREE • VEGETARIAN • VEGAN • SOY FREE • NUT FREE • EGG FREE

This butternut squash soup is silky smooth, savory with a touch of sweetness, and has a surprising pop of spice. It is just the right meal on a rainy or snowy day. Imagine enjoying a bowl while sitting in front of a roaring fire. One bite and you and your family will be craving this soup all winter long!

Yield 4 to 6 servings

To make this even easier and save you time, you can buy the squash already cleaned and cubed at many grocery stores. This takes care of the bulk of the chopping and lets you relax and let the pressure cooker do all the work!

1 large butternut squash

3 tablespoons (45 ml) olive or vegetable oil, divided

2 large shallots, minced

3 stalks celery, trimmed and finely chopped

2 carrots, trimmed and finely chopped

2 teaspoons (2 g) fresh thyme leaves

2 cloves garlic, minced

3 cups (705 ml) vegetable stock (page 214) or gluten-free store-bought stock, divided (see Note, page 61)

2 tablespoons (30 ml) maple syrup or agave syrup, or to taste

1 teaspoon kosher or fine sea salt

½ teaspoon freshly ground black pepper

¼ teaspoon hot sauce, or to taste (Sriracha brand is gluten free)

Chopped chives, for garnish

1 Place the squash in the microwave and heat for 1 to 2 minutes. This softens the rind and makes it easier and safer to cut. Using a large, sharp knife, cut the squash into quarters, scrape out the seeds and strings, and peel the chunks. Cut into cubes.

2 Press Sauté and add the oil to the inner pot. When it is hot, add the shallots, celery, carrots, and thyme and cook 4 minutes, stirring often, or until softened. Add the garlic and cook for 30 seconds. Add 1 cup (235 ml) of the stock to the pot, scraping the bottom to release any browned bits. Add the remaining 2 cups (470 ml) stock, maple syrup, salt, pepper, hot sauce, and butternut squash. Press Cancel.

3 Close and lock the lid, making sure the steam release handle is in the sealing position. Cook on high pressure for 9 minutes. When it is finished, release the pressure naturally for 10 minutes, then release the remaining pressure by turning the steam release handle to venting. When the pressure valve drops, unlock the lid and open it carefully. Check to make sure the squash is fork-tender. If it needs more time, replace the lid, return to pressure, and cook for another 2 or 3 minutes.

4 Use an immersion blender to puree the soup right in the inner pot, or transfer half of the soup at a time to a blender and puree in batches. Taste the soup and adjust the seasonings as needed. If the soup is too thick, add a little more stock or water. Ladle into serving bowls, sprinkle with the chives, and serve hot.

Black Bean Soup with Cilantro-Lime Cream

GLUTEN FREE • DAIRY-FREE OPTION • VEGETARIAN • VEGAN OPTION • SOY FREE • NUT FREE • EGG FREE

There are meals we experience in our lives that leave a lasting impression. The first time we had black bean soup was on a chilly afternoon at the renowned Chez Panisse in Berkeley, California. The soup had deeply layered flavors, and we loved the contrasting creaminess of the topping swirled into the soup. This black bean soup will fill you up and warm you on stormy days and with luck will help you create your own wonderful memories.

Yield About 6 servings

Note: If you forgot to soak the beans overnight, don't worry, you can still make the soup. Place the sorted beans in a sauce pot and add enough water to cover by 3 inches (7.6 cm). Bring to a boil and cook for 1 minute. Turn off the heat, cover, and let the beans rest for 1 hour. Drain and cook as directed above.

For the soup

16 ounces (454 g) dried black beans

2 tablespoons (30 ml) olive oil

1 large onion, finely chopped

1 large red bell pepper, cored, seeded, and finely chopped

2 stalks celery, trimmed and finely chopped

1 clove garlic, minced

1 tablespoon (3 g) dried oregano

1 tablespoon (6 g) ground cumin

1½ teaspoons kosher salt

½ teaspoon freshly ground black pepper

½ to 1 teaspoon chipotle powder, to taste

4 cups (940 ml) vegetable stock (page 214) or water, divided

Juice of ½ to 1 fresh lime

For the cilantro-lime cream (omit for dairy free and vegan)

¾ cup (180 g) sour cream

Juice of ½ to 1 fresh lime

¼ cup (4 g) fresh cilantro leaves, rinsed well and patted dry

½ to 1 teaspoon chipotle powder, to taste

Kosher or fine sea salt and ground white pepper, to taste

For optional garnishes

Chopped fresh cilantro leaves

Chopped scallion

Chopped ripe tomatoes

Fresh lime wedges

Soup

1 Sort the beans, discarding any pebbles or debris, rinse them well, and drain. Place in a large bowl and cover with fresh water. Loosely cover and set aside overnight. Drain before adding to the soup. (See Note.)

2 Press Sauté on your electric pressure cooker. Add the oil to the inner pot and when hot, add the onion, bell pepper, and celery. Cook, stirring often, until the vegetables have softened, about 4 minutes. Add the garlic, oregano, cumin, salt, pepper, and chipotle powder. Stir to evenly coat all the vegetables with the seasonings. Add 1 cup (235 ml) of the stock, scraping the bottom of the pot to release any browned bits. Pour in the remaining 3 cups (705 ml) stock and the soaked and drained black beans; stir well. Press Cancel.

3 Close and lock the lid, making sure the steam release handle is in the sealing position. Cook on high pressure for 12 minutes.

(continued)

*When you are working with
dried beans, be very careful to
check for small stones or bits of
rock. It is common to find some
in nearly every bag. Spread
the beans out on a baking sheet
with sides, which will contain
them. Working in sections,
sort through all of the beans,
discarding any debris you
find. Rinse the beans well and
drain before continuing with
the recipe.*

*Note: For information on
immersion blenders, see
page 79.*

Cilantro-Lime Cream

1 While the soup is cooking, make the cream. Combine the sour cream, lime juice (start with juice of ½ lime), cilantro, and chipotle powder in a food processor. Run the motor until the herbs are completely pureed and smooth. Taste and add salt and pepper. Add more lime juice or cilantro if you want a bolder, brighter flavor, but remember that flavors intensify over time. Transfer to a bowl and set aside while the soup finishes cooking.

Finish the Soup

1 When the soup is finished, release the pressure naturally for 10 minutes, then turn the steam release handle to venting, releasing any remaining steam. Unlock the lid and open it carefully.

2 Use an immersion blender to puree the soup or transfer to a blender and puree in batches. You can leave some of the beans whole for a chunkier texture or puree until completely smooth. Stir in the fresh lime juice. Taste and adjust the seasonings. Ladle into serving bowls, add a dollop of the cream (if using), and top with your desired garnishes. Serve immediately.

Vegetarian Minestrone

GLUTEN FREE • DAIRY FREE
• VEGETARIAN • VEGAN OPTION
• SOY FREE • NUT FREE • EGG FREE

Minestrone soup is found on the menus of Italian restaurants around the world. It is a delicious way for chefs and home cooks to use up the small bits of vegetables they have left over in their refrigerators. Feel free to use any vegetables you like and have on hand to make this rich and healthy soup.

Yield 4 to 6 servings

For the pasta

1 cup (105 g) uncooked rotini or elbow pasta, such as Barilla gluten-free brand

1 teaspoon kosher or fine sea salt

Olive or vegetable oil

For the soup

2 tablespoons (30 ml) olive or vegetable oil

1 large onion, finely chopped

2 large carrots, trimmed and chopped

2 stalks celery, trimmed and chopped

1 clove garlic, minced

2 teaspoons (1 g) dried oregano

1 teaspoon dried basil

1 bay leaf

1 (15-ounce, or 425 g) can chopped tomatoes (with their juices)

6 cups (1410 ml) vegetable stock (page 214)

½ teaspoon salt

¼ teaspoon freshly ground black pepper

3 zucchini, scrubbed, trimmed, and chopped

1 (15-ounce, or 425 g) can cannellini beans, rinsed and drained

Freshly grated Parmesan cheese (optional; omit for vegan)

Fresh basil, chopped, for garnish

If you want to make this ahead, make the soup portion but don't add the pasta, and store it in the refrigerator. The next day, cook the pasta, drain and lightly rinse, then add to the reheated soup. Gluten-free pasta does not reheat as well as regular pasta and is best when freshly cooked.

Pasta

1 Place the pasta and enough water to cover by 1 inch (2.5 cm) in the inner pot of your electric pressure cooker. Stir in the salt. Close and lock the lid, making sure the steam release handle is in the sealing position. Cook on high pressure for 2 minutes for rotini or 1 minute for elbows. Naturally release the pressure for 3 minutes, then quick release the remaining pressure by moving the handle to venting.

2 Unlock the lid and open it carefully. Pour the pasta into a colander, draining off any remaining cooking liquid. Rinse with cool water to stop the cooking, drain, toss with a little olive oil to prevent sticking, and set aside. Stir occasionally to keep the pieces separated.

Soup

1 Pour the oil into the inner pot of your electric pressure cooker. Press Sauté and heat the pot. When hot, add the onions, carrots, and celery. Cook, stirring often, until the onions are translucent, about 5 minutes. Stir in the garlic and cook for another minute. Stir in the oregano, basil, and bay leaf. Add the tomatoes and stock. Scrape the pot to loosen any browned bits. Stir in the salt and pepper. Press Cancel.

2 Close and lock the lid, making sure the steam release handle is in the sealing position. Cook on high pressure for 6 minutes. Naturally release the pressure for 3 minutes, then turn the steam release handle to venting. Unlock the lid and open it carefully. Stir in the zucchini and beans. Replace the lid and let sit for 4 minutes to cook the zucchini and heat the beans. Stir in the pasta and let sit for a minute or two to reheat.

3 Ladle the soup into bowls, and sprinkle the top with Parmesan cheese (if using) and fresh basil.

Note: The timing for the pasta may change depending on the brand of pasta you use. See page 98 for details.

Loaded Potato Leek Chowder

GLUTEN FREE • VEGETARIAN OPTION
• SOY FREE • NUT FREE • EGG FREE

Julia Child is an icon, and her legendary potato leek soup is the inspiration behind this soup. This version has become a wonderful chowder packed with chunky potatoes and luscious leeks (they look like large green onions), and topped with cheese and bacon. Enjoy every bite of this creamy soup with your favorite toppings.

Yield 4 servings

For the soup

6 thick slices gluten-free bacon, diced (Jones Dairy Farm brand is gluten free; omit for vegetarian)

2 leeks, light green and white parts only, trimmed, sliced into rings, and rinsed thoroughly

1 stalk celery, trimmed and finely chopped

1 large clove garlic, smashed, finely minced

2 teaspoons (1 g) dried thyme leaves

2 large russet potatoes, peeled and sliced

2 cups (470 ml) chicken stock (page 213) or vegetable stock (page 214)

1 cup (235 ml) water

½ teaspoon kosher or fine sea salt

Freshly ground black pepper, to taste

2 tablespoons (30 g) sour cream

½ cup (120 ml) heavy cream or half-and-half

For the garnishes

½ cup (60 g) shredded Gouda, cheddar, or any blend of cheeses

Chopped reserved cooked bacon

Finely chopped parsley

Minced red bell pepper

Finely chopped scallion or chives

Note: Make this a vegetarian soup by leaving out the bacon and replacing the rendered fat with 3 tablespoons (45 ml) olive oil. Use vegetable stock instead of chicken stock and add 1 ½ teaspoons of salt.

Soup

1 Press Sauté and heat the inner pot of your electric pressure cooker. Add the bacon and cook, stirring often, until crispy. Use a slotted spoon to transfer the bacon to a paper towel–lined plate. When cool enough to handle, chop finely.

2 Remove all but 3 tablespoons (45 ml) of the rendered fat from the inner pot (see Note for vegetarian option). Add the leeks, celery, and garlic to the pot. Cook, stirring often, until the leeks have softened, about 3 minutes. Add the thyme, potatoes, stock, and water, being sure there is nothing stuck to the bottom of the pot. Stir in the salt and pepper. Press Cancel.

3 Close and lock the lid, making sure the steam release handle is in the sealing position. Cook on high pressure for 5 minutes. When it is finished, release the pressure naturally for 6 minutes, and then quickly release the remaining pressure by turning the steam release handle to venting. It will take a while to release all the steam. When the floating pin drops, unlock the lid and open it carefully.

4 Transfer ½ cup (120 ml) of the soup to a bowl and whisk in the sour cream. Set aside. Use an immersion blender or potato masher to partially puree the rest of the soup and thicken it. Stir in the heavy cream and reserved sour cream mixture until completely incorporated. Taste and adjust the seasonings with salt and pepper as needed.

Garnishes

1 Ladle the soup into serving bowls and sprinkle a little of the cheese over the top of each bowl. Top with some of the bacon, parsley, red pepper, and scallions. Serve hot.

An immersion blender is an invaluable kitchen tool, allowing you to puree sauces and soups right in their cooking vessel without transferring to a blender. It is also amazingly good at making Hollandaise sauce from scratch.

4 GREAT GRAINS AND RICE

For centuries, whole grains have been feeding civilizations across the globe. They are a plentiful and inexpensive way to feed families. In addition to healthy fiber and nutrients, they add wonderful texture to your meals. One of the most challenging aspects of giving up gluten is losing favorite grains like barley, bulgur, and farro. Trying new-to-you grains can enhance your diet and help fill in the gaps left by gluten-full grains. Sorghum, millet, quinoa, and rice will have you reimagining what you think about when you hear the term *grains*.

Sorghum has a hearty, chewy texture and mild, nutty flavor that makes it perfect for use in pilafs, salads, and anywhere whole grains are on the ingredients list. It originated in Africa and is still a staple and source of nutrition in India and Africa. As a flour, it is a wonderful addition to gluten-free breads. It can even be popped like popcorn!

Millet was first cultivated nearly 10,000 years ago in China. It has a neutral, slightly sweet flavor and is a delicious alternative for salads, porridge, and stir-fries. When ground into a flour, it

enriches all of your baked goods. Quinoa, which is actually a seed, has gotten a lot of press lately and is becoming a go-to alternative grain. It has been a staple for thousands of years in the high reaches of the Andes Mountains in South America, and a sacred crop of the ancient Incans. High in fiber and protein, quinoa is a lovely option for vegetable salads and in soups. Rice comes in many different forms, giving you a multitude of textures, from soft and creamy to firm.

You are welcome to use these recipes as a guideline for how to make them in a pressure cooker as you reinterpret your family's favorites.

Recipes

Perfect Rice Every Time (White and Brown Varieties)

GLUTEN FREE • DAIRY FREE • VEGETARIAN • VEGAN • SOY FREE • NUT FREE • EGG FREE

All rice is not created equal. Each type—short grain, medium grain, or long grain—will cook slightly differently, so use these directions as a guide. This technique is designed for when you buy rice in bulk and where there are no directions to guide you. If you have a package with cooking directions on it, cut the cooking time in half and you will be very close to the right timing. Always make a note of changes so you can make adjustments the next time.

Yield 3 to 4 servings

For white rice

1 cup (180 g) long-grain white rice

1¼ cups (295 ml) water or vegetable stock (page 214)

½ teaspoon kosher or fine sea salt, or to taste

For brown rice

1 cup (190 g) brown rice

1½ cups (355 ml) water or vegetable stock (page 214)

½ teaspoon kosher or fine sea salt, or to taste

White Rice

1 Place the rice in a fine-mesh strainer and rinse under cold water until the water runs clear, about 1 minute. In the inner pot of your electric pressure cooker, stir together the rice, water, and salt. Close and lock the lid, making sure the steam release handle is in the sealing position. Cook on high pressure for 3 minutes.

2 When it is finished, release the pressure naturally for 12 minutes, then turn the steam release handle to venting, releasing any remaining steam. Unlock the lid and open it carefully. Use a fork to rake and fluff the rice before serving.

Brown Rice

1 Place the rice in a fine-mesh strainer and rinse under cold water until the water runs clear, about 1 minute. Stir together the rice, water, and salt in the inner pot of your electric pressure cooker. Close and lock the lid, making sure the steam release handle is in the sealing position. Cook on high pressure for 22 minutes.

2 When it is finished, release the pressure naturally for 10 minutes, then turn the steam release handle to venting, releasing any remaining steam. Unlock the lid and open it carefully. Use a fork to rake and fluff the rice before serving.

Although there is a "Rice" function on most of today's electric pressure cookers, they are mostly designed for white and converted rice. When cooking other types of rice, it is best to manually set the machine.

Brown Rice Pilaf

GLUTEN FREE • DAIRY FREE
• VEGETARIAN • VEGAN • SOY FREE
• NUT FREE • EGG FREE

A pilaf is both a technique and a dish. You coat the rice with oil and sauté it briefly before adding liquids and finishing the cooking. Cooking rice with vegetables and aromatics helps the taste penetrate deeply into each grain, creating intense flavor in every bite. This pilaf makes a beautiful side dish to any main course.

Yield 4 servings

Note: If you want to make this dish with white rice, it will take just 3 minutes. Decrease the vegetable stock to 1 cup (235 ml). The rest of the recipe remains the same.

2 tablespoons (30 ml) olive or vegetable oil

1 medium onion, finely chopped

1 red bell pepper, cored, seeded, and finely chopped

2 stalks celery, trimmed and finely chopped

2 carrots, peeled, trimmed, and finely chopped

1 cup (180 g) raw brown rice (see Note)

1 teaspoon minced garlic

¼ cup (60 ml) gluten-free dry white wine or water (see Note, page 133)

1¼ cups (295 ml) vegetable stock (page 214) or water

½ teaspoon dried thyme

½ teaspoon kosher or fine sea salt

¼ teaspoon freshly ground black pepper

1 Press Sauté on your electric pressure cooker. Heat the oil in the inner pot until shimmering. Add the onion, pepper, celery, and carrots. Cook, stirring often, until the onion is softened, about 3 minutes. Pour in the rice, stirring to coat all the grains with the oil. Continue cooking for about 5 minutes, or until the rice begins to smell nutty. Stir in the garlic and cook for 30 seconds. Add the wine, stirring to scrape up any browned bits from the bottom of the pot. Pour in the stock. Stir in the thyme, salt, and pepper. Press Cancel.

2 Close and lock the lid, making sure the steam release handle is in the sealing position. Cook on high pressure for 22 minutes. When it is finished, release the pressure naturally for 12 minutes, then turn the steam release handle to venting, releasing any remaining steam. Unlock the lid and open it carefully.

3 If there is any excess liquid present, press Sauté and cook the rice to evaporate it. Use a fork to fluff the rice. Taste and adjust the seasonings if needed. If it needs more cooking, replace the lid and let it rest for 5 minutes.

Quinoa Vegetable Salad with Lemon Vinaigrette

GLUTEN FREE • DAIRY FREE • VEGETARIAN • VEGAN • SOY FREE • NUT FREE • EGG FREE

This quinoa salad is packed with fresh seasonal vegetables and lightly dressed with a lemon vinaigrette. It is a great choice all year long, so feel free to use whatever vegetables are fresh and in season. If you are using very firm vegetables, such as cauliflower or broccoli, be sure to par-cook them first to soften them slightly.

Yield 4 to 6 servings

For the quinoa

1 cup (235 ml) vegetable stock (page 214) or water

¼ cup (60 ml) water

1 cup (175 g) quinoa, very well rinsed and drained

1 teaspoon kosher or fine sea salt

For the lemon vinaigrette

2 tablespoons (30 ml) freshly squeezed lemon juice

¼ cup (60 ml) extra virgin olive oil

1 teaspoon honey (or to taste)

½ teaspoon fresh thyme leaves

¼ teaspoon kosher or fine sea salt

⅛ teaspoon freshly ground black pepper

For the vegetables

1 tablespoon (15 ml) olive or vegetable oil

2 large carrots, trimmed and finely chopped

2 stalks celery, trimmed and finely chopped

1 large red bell pepper, cored, seeded, and finely chopped

2 tablespoons (20 g) minced red onion

1 cup (150 g) cherry tomatoes, quartered

1 medium cucumber, peeled, seeded, and finely chopped

2 scallions, trimmed and thinly sliced

2 teaspoons (1 g) fresh thyme leaves

Quinoa

1 Place the stock, water, quinoa, and salt in the inner pot of your electric pressure cooker. Stir and put the lid on the pot. Lock the lid, making sure the steam release handle is in the sealing position. Cook on high pressure for 4 minutes. When the quinoa is finished, let the pressure release naturally for 12 minutes, then turn the steam release handle to venting, releasing any remaining steam. Unlock the lid and open it carefully.

2 Transfer the quinoa to a bowl and set aside. Wipe out the pot and return to the pressure cooker.

(continued)

Quinoa's natural coating, called saponin, can make it taste bitter or soapy. Rinsing it well under cool running water will get rid of the coating and give you a pleasant-tasting grain to work with. Be sure to agitate the grains with your hands so all sides get equally rinsed.

Vinaigrette

1 While the quinoa is cooking, make the vinaigrette. In a bowl or jar with a tight lid, whisk together the dressing ingredients until emulsified. If using a jar, you can shake it vigorously to blend. Taste and adjust the seasonings as needed.

Vegetables

1 Press Sauté and heat the oil in the inner pot. Add the carrots, celery, bell pepper, and onion and cook, stirring often, until the onion is softened, about 3 minutes. Press Cancel.

2 Add the sautéed vegetables to the cooked quinoa. Stir in the tomatoes, cucumber, and scallion. Sprinkle the thyme over the top. Dress the salad with about 3 tablespoons (45 ml) of the vinaigrette, tossing to coat the grains and vegetables. Taste and adjust the seasonings, adding more vinaigrette if desired. Place the salad in the refrigerator and chill until ready to serve. The flavors will blend as it rests. Toss again before serving. Can be served cool or at room temperature.

Note: This quinoa salad is the perfect side dish for barbecues, showers, and dinner parties. Change some of the vegetables and herbs and you have a lovely option for your holiday celebrations. It is surprisingly filling and packed with protein, so it can also be served as a vegetarian/vegan main course. Flexibility makes this a wonderful choice all year long!

Savory Creamy Polenta

GLUTEN FREE • DAIRY-FREE OPTION • VEGETARIAN/VEGAN OPTION • SOY FREE • NUT FREE

Polenta is pure comfort food that can be served plain, sweetened, or as a base for savory meals. With brown sugar or maple syrup, it is the perfect way to start your day, and a great replacement for Cream of Wheat cereal. Topped with an Italian ragu, it is a luscious and filling meal. And it is a great side dish with grilled meats. This is another grain that takes a long time on the stove but quickly softens perfectly in your electric pressure cooker.

Yield About 4 servings

1 cup (164 g) polenta or medium-grind cornmeal

4 cups (940 ml) water or vegetable stock (page 214)

1 teaspoon kosher or fine sea salt

¼ cup (60 ml) heavy cream or half-and-half (optional)

½ cup (50 g) grated Parmesan cheese (optional)

1 Place the polenta, water, and salt in the inner pot of your electric pressure cooker. Stir well. Close and lock the lid, and make sure the steam release handle is in the sealing position before cooking on high for 5 minutes. When it is finished, allow the pressure to release naturally for 12 minutes. Then turn the steam release handle to venting, releasing any remaining steam. Unlock the lid and open it carefully.

2 Stir well with a whisk until the mixture becomes creamy and smooth, making sure to break up lumps. If desired, stir in the cream for additional richness. Scoop into bowls, sprinkle with the cheese, if using, and serve.

Notes: For a sweet version, use water and no cheese. Top bowls of cooked polenta with brown sugar or maple syrup just before serving.

Polenta and other cornmeal preparations will stick to the cooking pot if it is not immediately rinsed. Never wait too long to fill the pot with soapy water or your cleanup will be much more challenging.

Andouille and Chicken Jambalaya

GLUTEN FREE • DAIRY FREE • SOY FREE • NUT FREE • EGG FREE

Jambalaya is a long-standing food tradition in the American South, commonly enjoyed as part of classic New Orleans cuisine. This version is a rice dish that uses spicy sausage, chicken, tomatoes, and seasonings to dial up the heat and create a beautiful one-dish meal. It's perfect for Mardi Gras parties, but you can serve this all year long, and with electric pressure cookers, it is easy and quick to get on the table.

Yield 6 to 8 servings

Most recipes for jambalaya call for a "Cajun seasoning" mix. Unfortunately, many spice blends contain gluten or have cross-contamination issues. It may take a few minutes longer to make your own, but the payoff is better-tasting and safe-to-eat meals your whole family can enjoy.

1 tablespoon (15 ml) olive or vegetable oil

3 (1⅔ pounds, 815 g) boneless chicken breast halves, cut into ½-inch (1.3 cm) cubes

12 ounces (340 g) Cajun-style Andouille sausage, thinly sliced

1 large onion, finely diced

4 stalks celery, finely diced

2 green bell peppers, cored and finely diced

1½ cups (270 g) long-grain white rice, rinsed

2 bay leaves

2 teaspoons (1 g) dried thyme leaves

1 teaspoon dried oregano

1 teaspoon smoked paprika

½ teaspoon chipotle powder

1 teaspoon salt

½ teaspoon freshly ground black pepper

3 cloves garlic, minced

1½ cups (355 ml) chicken stock (page 213) or vegetable stock (page 214)

1 (14-ounce, or 392 g) can gluten-free crushed tomatoes

Chopped fresh parsley, for garnish

1 Press Sauté. When the inner pot is hot, pour in the oil. Add the chicken and cook for about 4 minutes, until partially cooked. Add the sausage, stirring often, for another 5 minutes, or until the chicken is cooked through. Transfer the meats to a bowl. Set aside.

2 Stir the onions, celery, and bell peppers into the inner pot. Cook until the vegetables have softened, about 8 minutes, stirring often. Add the rice and seasonings, stirring to coat the rice with the oil, then stir in the garlic. Cook for 30 seconds, stirring, until the garlic is fragrant. Press Cancel.

3 Pour in the stock, scraping the bottom of the pot to loosen any browned bits and rice.

Rice grains should be under the level of the liquid. Pour the tomatoes over the top but do not stir. Close and lock the lid, making sure the steam release handle is in the sealing position.

4 Cook on high pressure for 4 minutes. When finished, release the pressure naturally for 10 minutes, then quickly release remaining steam by turning the handle to the venting position. Unlock the lid and open it carefully.

5 Fluff the rice with two forks and then stir in the reserved chicken and sausage. Replace the lid and let rest for about 4 minutes, or until the meats are heated through. Scoop into serving bowls, sprinkle the tops with chopped parsley, and serve hot.

Saffron Risotto

GLUTEN FREE • DAIRY-FREE OPTION • VEGETARIAN • VEGAN OPTION • SOY FREE • NUT FREE • EGG FREE

The key to traditional risotto is constant stirring and adding the stock gradually. This makes it a very time-consuming task and one that can be intimidating to beginning cooks. Today's electric pressure cookers take all the guesswork out of making risotto and you no longer have to stand over the stove stirring while it cooks. You can use any seasonal vegetable in place of the peas if you like, such as asparagus, fava beans, zucchini, and so on. Cut them into small pieces and steam until just tender before adding to the dish.

Yield 4 servings

Saffron is a lovely, aromatic, and expensive spice. If you are looking for a less costly alternative, use ½ teaspoon turmeric in its place. Stir it into the rice after you've added the stock. It will add a pretty yellow hue and delicate flavor. It's not as fragrant as saffron, but still delicious.

½ teaspoon saffron threads

3 tablespoons (45 ml) boiling water

1 tablespoon (15 ml) olive or vegetable oil

½ medium onion, finely chopped

1 clove garlic, minced

1½ cups (285 g) Arborio or Carnaroli rice (do not substitute another style of rice)

2 tablespoons (30 ml) gluten-free dry white wine (optional; see Note, page 133)

1¾ cups (415 ml) water

2 cups (470 ml) vegetable stock (page 214), divided

½ teaspoon kosher or fine sea salt

¼ teaspoon freshly ground black pepper

2 tablespoons (28 g) unsalted butter or dairy-free/vegan alternative such as Earth Balance

1 teaspoon freshly grated lemon zest (optional)

1 cup (150 g) frozen peas

Grated Parmesan cheese (optional, omit for dairy free and vegan)

1 In a small bowl, soak the saffron in the hot water.

2 Press Sauté to heat the inner pot of your pressure cooker. Add the oil and heat until shimmering, then stir in the onion and garlic. Cook, stirring often, until the onion has softened slightly, about 4 minutes. Add the rice and stir to coat all the grains with the oil. Pour in the wine and cook until absorbed. Stir in the water, 1½ cups (355 ml) of the stock, the saffron with the soaking water, and the salt and pepper. Stir to make sure no browned bits are stuck on the bottom of the pot. Press Cancel.

3 Close and lock the lid, making sure the handle is in the sealing position. Cook for 4 minutes on high pressure. When it is finished, release the pressure naturally for 8 minutes, then turn the knob to the venting position and quickly release the remaining pressure. Unlock the lid and open it carefully.

4 Stir the rice until smooth and all the liquid has been incorporated. Stir in the butter until melted and the rice is creamy. Stir in the lemon zest and peas. Replace the lid and let the peas steam for 3 minutes. Taste and adjust the seasonings with more salt or pepper if needed. Toss the rice to evenly distribute the peas. If you want a creamier, looser texture, stir in the remaining ½ cup (120 ml) stock.

5 Ladle into bowls, sprinkle each with a little Parmesan cheese, if desired, and serve.

Creamy Parmesan Brown Rice

GLUTEN FREE • DAIRY-FREE OPTION
• VEGETARIAN • SOY FREE • NUT FREE
• EGG FREE

Similar in texture to risotto, this dish uses a short-grain brown rice for a chewy texture that enhances every bite. Rich and cheesy, it is an excellent side dish for grilled meats or makes a delicious vegetarian main course. The saltiness of the stock and Parmesan should be enough for the entire dish, but if needed you can sprinkle with some coarse salt before serving.

Yield 4 servings

2 tablespoons (30 ml) olive or vegetable oil

1 medium onion, finely diced

1 carrot, trimmed and finely diced

1 red bell pepper, seeded and finely diced

2 teaspoons (1 g) fresh thyme leaves or 1 teaspoon dried thyme

1 teaspoon dried oregano

1 cup (180 g) short-grain brown rice, such as Lundberg Family Farms brand

¼ cup (60 ml) gluten-free dry white wine or water (see Note, page 133)

1¼ cups (295 ml) vegetable stock (page 214) or water, plus more if needed

½ teaspoon salt

¼ to ½ teaspoon freshly ground black pepper

¼ cup (35 g) frozen peas

½ cup (50 g) grated Parmesan or (60 g) Monterey Jack cheese or dairy-free cheese

1 Press Sauté on your electric pressure cooker. Add the oil and heat until shimmering. Add the onion, carrot, and bell pepper and cook, stirring, until the onion is softened, about 3 minutes. Stir in the thyme and oregano, and then stir in the rice, making sure that all the grains are coated with the oil. Add the wine and cook until it is absorbed by the rice, stirring constantly. Be sure there are no browned bits stuck to the bottom of the pot. Pour in the stock and add the salt and pepper. Press Cancel.

2 Close and lock the lid, making sure the steam release handle is in the sealing position. Cook on high pressure for 23 minutes. When it is finished, release the pressure naturally for 12 minutes, then turn the steam release handle to venting. When the float pin drops, unlock the lid and open it carefully.

3 Stir the peas into the rice and sprinkle the Parmesan over the top. Replace the lid, and let rest for about 3 minutes to cook the peas and melt the cheese. If you want a creamier consistency, stir in a little more stock. Taste and adjust the seasonings if needed. Serve immediately.

Millet Tabbouleh

GLUTEN FREE • DAIRY FREE •
VEGETARIAN • VEGAN • SOY FREE •
NUT FREE • EGG FREE

Tabbouleh, a national dish of Lebanon, is traditionally made with bulgur wheat. For this recipe we use millet in its place. Millet is a lovely and underutilized gluten-free grain. With a subtle flavor and pale yellow color, it is a nice change-of-pace grain. Packed with fresh herbs and vegetables, this tabbouleh is perfect for a light lunch or brunch, a vegetarian main course, or a wonderful accompaniment to grilled foods all summer long.

Yield 4 to 6 servings

For the millet

1 cup (175 g) whole-grain millet, rinsed well and drained

2 cups (470 ml) cool water

1 teaspoon kosher or fine sea salt

For the tabbouleh

1 cup (100 g) minced scallion

¼ cup (24 g) finely chopped fresh mint leaves

¼ cup (15 g) finely chopped fresh flat-leaf parsley

1 cucumber, peeled, split length-wise, and seeds scraped out, finely diced

2 cups (300 g) cherry tomatoes, quartered and drained in a strainer

1 teaspoon kosher or fine sea salt

½ teaspoon freshly ground black pepper

For the dressing

¼ cup (60 ml) extra virgin olive oil

2 tablespoons (30 ml) freshly squeezed lemon juice

¼ to ½ teaspoon honey

¼ teaspoon kosher or fine sea salt

⅛ teaspoon freshly ground black pepper

Millet

1 Place the millet, water, and salt in the inner pot of your electric pressure cooker. Close and lock the lid, making sure the steam release handle is in the sealing position. Cook on high pressure for 9 minutes. When it is finished, release the pressure naturally for 10 minutes, then turn the steam release handle to venting, releasing any remaining steam. Unlock the lid and open it carefully.

2 If there is any excess water, pour the millet into a fine-mesh strainer to drain. Transfer to a large bowl and set aside to cool to room temperature, tossing and raking it occasionally with two forks to ensure it doesn't clump.

Tabbouleh

1 Add the scallions, mint, parsley, cucumbers, tomatoes, salt, and pepper to the millet. Toss to combine.

Dressing

1 In a bowl, whisk together the oil and lemon juice until emulsified. Whisk in the honey, salt, and pepper. Taste and adjust the seasonings if needed, then drizzle half over the salad. Toss to coat everything with the dressing. Cover and let rest for at least 30 minutes before tasting and adjusting the seasonings. Add more dressing if desired. Serve at room temperature. Store, covered, in the refrigerator.

Millet and Chicken Greek Salad

GLUTEN FREE • DAIRY-FREE OPTION •
SOY FREE • NUT FREE • EGG FREE

Millet is a gluten-free grain that is similar to couscous or quinoa, with a touch of nuttiness in every bite. When combined with these Greek-inspired ingredients, it makes a delightful salad that wakes up your taste buds and is perfect for summer picnics or potlucks all year long.

Yield About 4 servings

For the salad

2 tablespoons (30 ml) vegetable or olive oil

½ cup (80 g) very finely chopped onion

1 red bell pepper, cored, seeded, and very finely chopped

1 cup (175 g) millet, rinsed well and drained

½ teaspoon kosher or fine sea salt

½ teaspoon freshly ground black pepper

1 teaspoon dried oregano

1 cup (235 ml) water

¾ cup (180 ml) chicken stock (page 213) or water

1½ cups (60 g) baby spinach leaves, rinsed very well, shaken dry

1 small cucumber, peeled and finely chopped

⅓ cup (35 g) chopped olives, preferably Kalamata

⅓ cup (50 g) quartered cherry tomatoes

½ small red onion, very thinly sliced

1½ cups (210 g) cooked chicken (see page 128), cut into small cubes or shredded, at room temperature

For the dressing

⅓ cup (80 ml) extra virgin olive oil

2 tablespoons (30 ml) freshly squeezed lemon juice

1 to 2 tablespoons (15 to 30 ml) red wine vinegar, to taste

½ teaspoon kosher or fine sea salt

¼ teaspoon freshly ground black pepper

For topping

2 tablespoons (6 g) finely chopped fresh parsley

¼ cup (38 g) crumbled feta cheese (optional)

(continued)

Salad

1 Press Sauté and heat the vegetable oil in the inner pot of your electric pressure cooker. When it is shimmering, add the chopped onion and bell pepper and cook, stirring, for 4 minutes, or until the onion is slightly softened. Add the millet. Sprinkle with the salt, pepper, and oregano, then pour in the water and stock, stirring to be sure nothing is stuck to the bottom of the pot. Press Cancel.

2 Close and lock the lid, making sure the steam release handle is in the sealing position. Cook on high pressure for 9 minutes. When it is finished, release the pressure naturally for 8 minutes, then turn the steam release handle to venting, releasing any remaining steam. Unlock the lid and open it carefully.

3 Remove the lid, rake the grains with a fork, and transfer to a large bowl. Add the spinach to the bowl, stir it into the millet, and let the steam wilt the greens. Set aside to cool to room temperature, tossing occasionally with forks to help keep the millet from clumping. When cooled, stir in the cucumber, olives, tomatoes, red onion, and chicken.

Dressing

1 In a small bowl, whisk together the olive oil, lemon juice, vinegar, salt, and pepper. Pour half the dressing over the salad, tossing to coat all the ingredients. Taste and adjust the seasonings; add the remaining dressing if desired and toss again. Sprinkle the parsley and feta over the top and serve.

Brown and Wild Rice Pilaf with Mushrooms and Snow Peas

GLUTEN FREE • DAIRY FREE • VEGETARIAN • VEGAN • SOY FREE • NUT FREE • EGG FREE

Full of luscious flavors and textures, this pilaf is substantial enough to be a vegetarian main course, or serve it as a delightful side dish. The cranberries add a pop of fresh, bright flavor in every bite. Commercial rice blends come with a variety of ingredients and variable cooking times. Be sure to check the packaging to see what the recommended cook time is and halve it for this recipe.

Yield 6 to 8 servings

2 tablespoons (30 ml) olive or vegetable oil, divided

1 shallot, thinly sliced

4 ounces (115 g) snow peas, strings removed, thinly sliced

6 large mushrooms, sliced

½ cup (75 g) dried sweetened cranberries

¼ cup (40 g) finely chopped onion

2 cups (360 g) brown and wild rice blend

½ cup (120 ml) gluten-free dry white wine or more stock (see Note, page 133)

1 cup (235 ml) vegetable stock (page 214), chicken stock (page 213), or water

1 cup (235 ml) water

½ teaspoon kosher or fine sea salt

½ teaspoon freshly ground black pepper

½ cup (55 g) sliced almonds

1 Press Sauté on your pressure cooker and add 1 tablespoon (15 ml) of the oil to the inner pot. Add the shallots, snow peas, and mushrooms. Cook, stirring often, until the shallots are softened, about 2 minutes. Use a slotted spoon to transfer the vegetables to a bowl. Stir in the cranberries and set aside.

2 With the pressure cooker still on Sauté, pour the remaining 1 tablespoon (15 ml) oil in the inner pot. Add the onion and cook until softened, about 4 minutes. Add the rice and toss to coat each grain with the oil. Add the wine to the pot and scrape the bottom to loosen any browned bits. Add the stock, water, salt, and pepper, stirring. Close and lock the lid, making sure the steam release handle is in the sealing position. Cook on high pressure for half the time listed on the rice package, about 20 minutes.

3 When it is finished, release the pressure naturally, about 12 minutes. Turn the steam release handle to venting, releasing any remaining steam. When the float pin drops, unlock the lid and open it carefully.

4 Stir in the reserved vegetables and any accumulated juices, replace the lid, and let rest for about 4 minutes. When the vegetables are reheated, remove the lid and use a fork to fluff the rice and distribute the vegetables evenly. If there is excess liquid, leave it on Keep Warm or press Sauté (set to low) for a few minutes with the lid off and it will evaporate. Scoop portions onto plates, sprinkle with the almonds, and serve.

5 PLENTIFUL PASTA

Pasta is one of the most missed foods when you have to eat gluten free. Thankfully, there are a number of good-quality products now available to us.

Everyone will have preferences, and you can certainly use what you like, but for consistency while testing the recipes, we settled on a single brand: Barilla gluten-free pasta. We tested a lot of brands while researching this book, and Barilla gluten-free pasta is most readily available in the United States. It gives us consistently good results and holds up to pressure cooking. If it isn't available in your area, you can buy it online. Other brands will likely work but may require different cooking times and may be more fragile.

We found that a blend of rice and corn in gluten-free pasta varieties provides the best of both worlds—good flavor and texture. Gluten-free pastas are more delicate than traditional wheat-based pasta. For this reason, in most cases we cook the pasta first, set it aside while we make the sauce or other steps, then add it back at the end to reheat. This keeps it from getting overcooked and mushy.

A general rule of thumb when cooking gluten-free pasta in the pressure cooker is to cut the recommended cook time in half and then take another minute or two off. Do a controlled pressure release, which means you hold the steam release handle and slowly let the steam out to reduce spewing starchy water all over your kitchen. This stops the cooking more quickly than a natural pressure release. If you are using another brand of pasta, the timing may be different. And different brands may behave differently, so try the recipe as written, and then make adjustments as needed. Enjoy having pasta again!

Recipes

Luscious Mac and Cheese with Crispy Bacon

GLUTEN FREE • VEGETARIAN OPTION •
SOY FREE • NUT FREE • EGG FREE

Mac and cheese is the supreme comfort food, especially beloved by children. Pasta covered with a tempting cheesy sauce is heavenly and something you miss terribly when you can no longer eat gluten. But thanks to the development of good-quality gluten-free pasta, we can make a safe version of our childhood favorite. And if you add it, the bacon lends wonderful flavor and terrific texture on top.

Yield About 4 servings

Note: The timing for the pasta may change depending on the brand of pasta you use. See page 98 for details.

4 slices gluten-free bacon, chopped (optional, replace with 2 tablespoons [30 ml] oil for vegetarian)

½ small onion, grated

3¾ cups (880 ml) water

12 ounces (340 g) uncooked elbow macaroni, such as Barilla gluten-free brand

1½ teaspoons kosher or fine sea salt

1 (12-ounce, or 340 g) can evaporated milk (*not* sweetened condensed) or whole milk

1 teaspoon dry mustard powder

1 teaspoon black pepper

½ teaspoon nutmeg (optional)

24 ounces (672 g) shredded extra-sharp cheddar cheese

8 ounces (227 g) shredded fontina or Monterey Jack cheese

2 ounces (56 g) grated Parmesan cheese

Hot pepper sauce, to taste (optional) (Sriracha brand is gluten free)

1 Press Sauté on your electric pressure cooker. When hot, add the bacon to the inner pot and cook, stirring, until crisp. Transfer to a paper towel–lined plate to cool. Remove all but 2 tablespoons (30 ml) of the fat from the inner pot. Add the onion and cook, stirring, until fully softened, about 5 minutes. Press Cancel.

2 Add the water, pasta, and salt to the inner pot. Stir and make sure the pasta is completely covered with the liquid. Close and lock the lid, making certain the steam release handle is in the sealing position. Cook on high pressure for 1 minute.

3 When it is finished, release the pressure naturally for 4 minutes, then slowly vent the remaining pressure by moving the handle between venting and sealing, letting out a little steam at a time. Use a hot pad to protect your hand. When all the steam is released, unlock the lid and open it carefully.

4 Test the pasta; it should be just tender and not too chewy. It will continue cooking as you finish making the dish. If it needs more time, set the lid back on the pressure cooker and let it rest for a few minutes.

5 Stir the milk, mustard powder, pepper, and nutmeg into the cooked pasta. Mix until evenly distributed. Add the cheeses, a little at a time, stirring until melted and creamy before adding more. Add a little hot pepper sauce if desired. If the sauce gets too thick, add ¼ cup (60 ml) hot water or more to thin. Taste and adjust the seasonings if needed. Crumble the bacon and sprinkle on top; serve immediately.

Creamy Pesto Pasta

GLUTEN FREE • VEGETARIAN • SOY FREE • EGG FREE

This dish began with the memory of a recipe made decades ago, a lush cheesy pesto pasta dish. In this new version, oodles of pesto-coated pasta and mascarpone cheese come together in a delightful casserole that can be a side dish or vegetarian main course. One bite and you know this easy and delicious pasta will become an instant family favorite.

Yield 2 to 3 servings

Note: The timing for the pasta may change depending on the brand of pasta you use. See page 98 for details.

8 ounces (227 g) rotini pasta, such as Barilla gluten-free brand

1 teaspoon kosher or fine sea salt

1 tablespoon (15 ml) olive or vegetable oil

¼ cup (60 g) gluten-free pesto sauce, such as Buitoni or Trader Joe's brands, or more to taste

8 ounces (227 g) mascarpone cheese

¼ cup (25 g) grated Parmesan cheese

1½ cups (355 ml) water for the bottom of the pot

1 Place the pasta in the inner pot of your electric pressure cooker and add water to cover. Stir in the salt and add the olive oil to the water to help prevent sticking.

2 Close and lock the lid, making sure the steam release handle is in the sealing position. Cook on high pressure for 1 minute. When it is finished, release the pressure naturally for 4 minutes. Then hold the steam release handle halfway between sealing and venting (use a hot pad to protect your hand) until all the steam is released. Unlock the lid and open it carefully. Press Cancel. Pour the pasta into a colander and drain well.

3 In a large mixing bowl, stir together the pesto and mascarpone until smooth. Add the pasta to the pesto mixture and stir until all the pieces are evenly coated.

4 Butter a 7-inch (18 cm) round baking pan and line the bottom with parchment paper. Place the pesto-coated pasta in the pan. Sprinkle the Parmesan on top. Place a square of foil over the pan, crimping around the edges of the pan.

5 Wipe out the inner pot. Pour in 1½ cups (355 ml) water and place a trivet in the bottom. Set the pan on a sling (see page 18) and place it on the trivet. Close and lock the lid, making sure the steam release handle is in the sealing position. Cook on high pressure for 2 minutes. When it is finished, release the pressure naturally for 5 minutes, then quickly release the remaining steam. Unlock the lid and open it carefully. Press Cancel.

6 Lift the pan out of the pot and set it on a wire cooling rack. Carefully lift the foil off the pan. If you want some color on the top, slip the pan under the broiler for a few minutes until the cheese is bubbling and browned in spots. Let rest for 5 minutes before scooping out servings.

Shrimp and Pasta in a Lemon Cream Sauce

GLUTEN FREE • SOY FREE • NUT FREE • EGG FREE

There is an Italian restaurant in the San Francisco Bay Area that serves pasta in a lemon cream sauce that is always a popular menu item. This recipe's combination of shrimp, dill, lemon, and pasta is a lovely, light yet satisfying meal that would be perfect for luncheons, showers, or brunches. It comes together very quickly and you will have dinner on the table in no time.

Yield 4 servings

Shrimp come in a variety of sizes, and each will take a different amount of time to cook. You want to cook them in batches so every piece touches the bottom of the pot. When both sides are pink and opaque, remove from the heat and place in a bowl. Continue cooking the remaining shrimp until they are all just done. Cover the bowl and the residual heat will finish cooking them through.

For the pasta

12 ounces (340 g) penne pasta, such as Barilla gluten-free brand

1 teaspoon kosher or fine sea salt

Olive oil, for tossing

For the shrimp

1 tablespoon (15 ml) olive or vegetable oil

1 medium shallot, minced

1½ pounds (680 g) raw medium shrimp, peeled and deveined

½ teaspoon minced fresh dill

Kosher or fine sea salt and freshly ground black pepper, to taste

For the lemon cream sauce

3 tablespoons (42 g) butter

1½ cups (355 ml) heavy cream or evaporated milk

1½ cloves garlic, peeled

2 teaspoons (10 ml) freshly squeezed lemon juice

2 teaspoons (4 g) finely grated lemon zest

1¼ cups (125 g) grated Parmesan cheese, divided

Salt and freshly ground black pepper, to taste

Finely chopped fresh Italian parsley or chives, for garnish

Pasta

1 Place the pasta in the inner pot of your pressure cooker. Pour in enough water to cover the pasta by 1 inch (2.5 cm). Stir the pasta to make sure it doesn't stick to the bottom of the pan. Sprinkle the salt in the water. Close and lock the lid, making sure the steam release handle is in the sealing position. Cook on high pressure for 2 minutes.

2 When it is finished, release the pressure naturally for 3 minutes, then do a controlled release by turning the steam release handle to halfway between sealing and venting positions. Protect your hand with a hot pad. When all the steam has been released, press Cancel. Unlock the lid and open it carefully. Pour the pasta into a colander, drain it, and toss with a little oil to keep it from sticking together as it sits. Wipe out the inner pot.

Shrimp

1 Press Sauté and heat the inner pot. Add the oil and when hot, stir in the shallot. Cook for about 1 minute, until just beginning to color. Add half the shrimp and dill, tossing to coat with the oil. Cook, stirring often, until the shrimp become opaque and turn pink on both sides, 1 to 2 minutes on each side, until just done. Sprinkle lightly with salt and pepper. Use a slotted spoon to scoop the shrimp out of the pot and add to the pasta; cover to keep warm. Repeat with the remaining shrimp and dill.

Lemon Cream Sauce

1 Add the butter to the inner pot, warming until fully melted. Whisk in the cream, garlic, lemon juice, and zest. Cook until warmed, whisking often to avoid scorching. Discard the garlic. Whisk in 1 cup (100 g) of the Parmesan cheese until smooth. Press Cancel. Taste and adjust the seasonings with salt and pepper if needed.

2 Add the pasta and shrimp to the sauce, tossing to thoroughly coat each piece. Replace the lid and let it rest for a couple of minutes, or until the pasta and shrimp are heated through. Add a splash of water if the sauce gets too thick.

3 To serve, scoop the pasta and shrimp into bowls and sprinkle the top of each serving with 1 tablespoon (6 g) of the remaining Parmesan cheese and a little parsley. Serve hot.

Note: The timing for the pasta may change depending on the brand of pasta you use. See page 98 for details.

Chicken Tetrazzini with Rotini

GLUTEN FREE • SOY FREE • EGG FREE • NUT FREE

Chicken tetrazzini is a wonderful old-fashioned American comfort food, guaranteed to be greeted with delight by your entire family. We've found ways to easily make a gluten-free version, perfect for family gatherings, parties, or weeknight meals. We've designed a new family favorite just for you—enjoy!

Yield About 4 servings

Note: The timing for the pasta may change depending on the brand of pasta you use. See page 98 for details.

1 tablespoon (15 ml) olive oil

2 pounds (908 g) boneless, skinless chicken breasts, cut into bite-size pieces

2 tablespoons (28 g) unsalted butter

1 yellow onion, chopped

2 cloves garlic, minced

4¼ cups (1 L) chicken stock (page 213), divided

1 tablespoon (2 g) fresh thyme leaves

2 teaspoons (6 g) smoked paprika

1 cup (235 ml) milk

12 ounces (340 g) rotini pasta, such as Barilla gluten-free brand

6 ounces (168 g) cream cheese, softened and cut into pieces

1 cup (100 g) freshly grated Parmesan cheese, plus more for serving

1 cup (150 g) frozen peas

½ cup (35 g) sliced button mushrooms

½ cup (30 g) chopped fresh parsley, for garnish

1 Press Sauté on your electric pressure cooker. When the inner pot is hot, add the olive oil. Add the chicken to the oil and brown lightly on each side. Remove the chicken from the pot and set aside.

2 Add the butter and onions to the pot. Sauté for 2 minutes, or until soft. Add the garlic and cook for an additional 30 seconds, until fragrant.

3 Add 1 cup (235 ml) of the chicken stock to the pot, scraping the bottom of the pot to deglaze it. Return the chicken to the pot. Add the remaining 3¼ cups (765 ml) stock, thyme, paprika, milk, and pasta.

4 Close and lock the lid, making sure the steam release handle is in the sealing position. Cook on high pressure for 5 minutes. When the cook time is finished, press Cancel. Do a quick pressure release by carefully moving the sealing handle to venting and allowing all the steam to escape. When the float pin drops, unlock the lid and open it carefully.

5 Add the cream cheese pieces and stir gently until all the cheese is melted and the sauce is smooth. Stir in the Parmesan, peas, and mushrooms. Return the lid to the pot and allow to sit in the residual heat for 2 to 4 minutes, or until the peas are warmed through. The sauce will thicken as it cools, so be sure to stir it well before serving.

6 To serve, place in pretty bowls and garnish with plenty of parsley on top and extra Parmesan if needed!

Pork Tenderloin Marsala and Penne Pasta

GLUTEN FREE • DAIRY FREE • SOY FREE • NUT FREE • EGG FREE

This Italian dish is usually served with chicken or veal, but we thought it would be fun to try it with a pork tenderloin. The slight sweetness of the wine is a beautiful accompaniment to the pork. The meat is incredibly moist and tender, and the sauce is rich and indulgent. This can be served for special occasions or, because the pork cooks so quickly, for weeknight dinners.

Yield 3 to 4 servings

8 ounces (227 g) penne pasta, such as Barilla gluten-free brand

2 teaspoons (12 g) kosher or fine sea salt, plus more to taste

2 tablespoons (30 ml) olive or vegetable oil, divided, plus more for drizzling

1 (about 1½-pound, or 680 g) pork tenderloin

4 slices pancetta or bacon, chopped

1 small onion, finely chopped

1 clove garlic, minced

8 ounces (227 g) cremini or button mushrooms, stemmed and halved or quartered

¾ cup (180 ml) sweet Marsala wine (see Note, page 133) or chicken stock (page 213)

¼ cup (60 ml) chicken stock (page 213)

Several sprigs fresh thyme

2 tablespoons (16 g) cornstarch (see page 24 for more information on thickeners)

3 tablespoons (45 ml) cool water

Kosher salt and freshly ground black pepper, as needed

Minced fresh parsley, for garnish

1 Place the penne in the inner pot of your electric pressure cooker. Fill the pot with fresh water to cover by 1 inch (2.5 cm). Stir to make sure the pasta isn't sticking to the bottom of the pan. Sprinkle the salt in the water. Close and lock the lid, making sure the steam release handle is in the sealing position. Cook on high pressure for 2 minutes. When it is finished, release the pressure naturally for 3 minutes, then do a controlled release by holding the handle halfway between the sealing and venting positions. Protect your hand with a hot pad. When all the steam has been released, press Cancel.

2 Unlock the lid and open it carefully. Pour the pasta into a colander and drain. Drizzle with a little oil and toss to keep it from sticking together as it sits. Set aside and stir occasionally.

3 Press Sauté and heat 1 tablespoon (15 ml) of the oil in the inner pot. When shimmering, add the pork tenderloin. Brown for about 3 minutes on each side. Transfer the pork to a plate and tent with foil to help keep warm.

4 Add the remaining 1 table-spoon (15 ml) oil to the pot. Stir in the pancetta and cook until slightly crispy, about 4 minutes, stirring often. Use a slotted spoon to transfer the pancetta to a bowl. Remove all but 2 tablespoons (30 ml) of the fat. Add the onion to the pot and cook for 3 minutes, stirring, until softened. Stir in the garlic, cook for 30 seconds, then stir in the mushrooms. Cook, stirring often, for 2 minutes.

5 Pour in the Marsala wine and chicken stock. Scrape the bottom of the pan to loosen any browned bits. Transfer the pork and its juices back to the pot, nestling it into the liquid. Sprinkle in the cooked pancetta. Close and lock the lid, making sure the steam release handle is in the sealing position.

6 Cook on high pressure for 5 minutes. When it is finished, release the pressure naturally for 7 minutes, then turn the steam release handle to venting, releasing remaining steam. Unlock the lid and open it carefully. Press Cancel. Remove the pork from the pot, check to make sure it has reached at least 145°F (63°C) in the center with an instant-read thermometer (if it needs more time, return it to the pot and let rest in the heat for a few minutes longer), place on a cutting board, cover, and keep warm.

7 Add the thyme to the pot. In a small bowl, whisk the corn-starch and water together until fully dissolved. Press Sauté and whisk the cornstarch slurry into the cooking liquid in the pot. Cook, whisking constantly, until it comes to a boil and thickens. Taste and adjust the seasonings with salt and pepper if needed.

8 Stir the pasta into the sauce and return the tenderloin to the pot. Replace the lid and let rest for 1 to 2 minutes to rewarm the pasta. Press Cancel.

9 Cut the pork into thick slices. Divide the pork between plates, add some of the pasta, top with the sauce and mushrooms, sprinkle with the parsley, and serve hot.

Note: The timing for the pasta may change depending on the brand of pasta you use. See page 98 for details.

Penne all' Amatriciana

GLUTEN FREE • DAIRY-FREE OPTION •
VEGETARIAN OPTION • SOY FREE • NUT
FREE • EGG FREE

Marinara sauce is the simplest tomato-based Italian pasta sauce, but your taste buds will jump for joy when you take a bite of this spicier version with red pepper flakes and chopped pancetta. Leave out the pepper flakes if you have sensitive folks or children at your table. Did you know each pasta shape has a purpose? The shape of the penne helps hold the sauce, giving you more flavor in every bite.

Yield About 4 servings

For the pasta

8 ounces (227 g) penne pasta, such as Barilla gluten-free brand

2 teaspoons (12 g) salt

Olive or vegetable oil

For the sauce

1 tablespoon (15 ml) olive or vegetable oil

8 ounces (227 g) pancetta or gluten-free unsmoked bacon, chopped (omit for vegetarian)

1 medium onion, thinly sliced

2 cloves garlic, thinly sliced

1 teaspoon red pepper flakes, or to taste

¼ cup (60 ml) dry white wine (see Note, page 133)

½ cup (120 ml) water

1½ cups (355 ml) tomato sauce or crushed tomatoes, such as Pomi brand

Kosher or fine sea salt and freshly ground black pepper, to taste

2 tablespoons (5 g) chopped basil leaves

1 teaspoon dried oregano

2 tablespoons (7 g) finely chopped parsley, for garnish

Grated Parmesan or Pecorino Romano cheese, for garnish (use dairy-free cheese for dairy-free)

Note: The timing for the pasta may change depending on the brand of pasta you use. See page 98 for details.

Pasta

1 Place the pasta in the inner pot of your electric pressure cooker and add water to cover by 1 inch (2.5 cm). Sprinkle the salt over the top and add a splash of oil. Close and lock the lid, making sure the steam release handle is in the sealing position. Cook on high pressure for 2 minutes. When it is finished, release the pressure naturally for 3 minutes, and then quickly release the remaining pressure by turning the steam release handle to venting. Press Cancel.

2 Unlock the lid and open it carefully. Pour the pasta into a colander and drain. Drizzle with a little more oil to keep the pieces from sticking as they sit, tossing to coat each piece. Stir occasionally while the sauce cooks.

Sauce

1 Press Sauté and heat the inner pot of your electric pressure cooker. Add the oil and stir in the pancetta. Cook, stirring often, until starting to get crispy, about 3 minutes. Use a slotted spoon to transfer the pancetta to a paper towel–lined plate. Remove all but 1 tablespoon (15 ml) of the drippings.

2 Add the onion to the pot and cook, stirring, until softened, about 3 minutes. Add the garlic, red pepper flakes, and wine. Stir, scraping up any browned bits on the bottom of the pan, and cook until nearly evaporated, a couple of minutes. Pour in the water and tomato sauce, and season with salt and pepper. Bring to a boil and cook for 5 minutes to concentrate the sauce a bit, stirring often. Stir in the basil, oregano, and cooked pancetta. Press Cancel. Stir in the cooked pasta, replace the lid, and let rest for about 3 minutes until the pasta has been reheated.

3 Serve, sprinkling the top of each bowl with a little of the parsley and passing the cheese at the table.

Classic Lasagna with Meat Sauce

GLUTEN FREE • SOY FREE • NUT FREE • EGG FREE

Cheesy, meaty, and totally satisfying, this lasagna is a real family favorite. This casserole can be made ahead and frozen to have on hand for busy nights, or you can make a second lasagna if you are feeding a larger crowd. If you don't want to make the meat sauce, you can use a homemade marinara sauce or, if time is tight, your favorite gluten-free jarred pasta sauce works well, too. Some brands we like that have gluten-free varieties include Barilla, Amy's Kitchen, Rao's, Classico, and Muir Glen Organic. Always read the labels to make sure the brand and flavor you choose is gluten free, as manufacturers can change their production practices without notice.

Yield About 4 servings

For the meat sauce

1 tablespoon (15 ml) olive or vegetable oil

½ pound (227 g) ground beef

½ pound (227 g) ground pork (*not* sausage)

1 medium onion, finely chopped

2 cloves garlic, minced

2 cups (480 g) gluten-free crushed or strained tomatoes, such Pomi brand

1 tablespoon (3 g) dried oregano

¼ teaspoon whole fennel seeds

2 teaspoons (12 g) kosher or fine sea salt

½ teaspoon freshly ground black pepper

For the cheese mixture

1 cup (240 g) ricotta cheese

½ cup (50 g) grated Parmesan cheese

2 tablespoons (5 g) chopped fresh basil leaves

2 teaspoons (1 g) dried oregano

½ teaspoon kosher or fine sea salt

½ teaspoon freshly ground black pepper

For assembly

½ (10-ounce, or 283 g) box oven-ready lasagna noodles, such as Barilla gluten-free brand

1½ cups (180 g) shredded mozzarella cheese

¼ cup (25 g) grated Parmesan cheese

Extra chopped basil leaves, for garnish

For the cooking pot

1½ cups (355 ml) water

1 Line the bottom of a 7-inch (18 cm) round springform pan or push pan (like you use to make cheesecake) with parchment paper. Line the sides with a strip of parchment. Wrap the bottom of the pan with a sheet of foil to contain any liquids. Set aside.

Meat Sauce

1 Press Sauté on your electric pressure cooker. Add the oil to the inner pot and brown the meats. Use a spoon or flat-edged spatula to break up clumps, making the pieces as small as you can. Add the onion and garlic and cook, stirring, until the onion is softened, about 4 minutes. Stir in the tomatoes, oregano, fennel seeds, salt, and pepper. Simmer for about 5 minutes to blend the flavors. Taste the sauce and add more salt or pepper if needed. Pour into a bowl. Clean the inner pot.

Cheese Mixture

1 In a bowl, stir together the ricotta cheese, Parmesan, basil, oregano, salt, and pepper with a fork until smooth.

Assembly

1 Cover the bottom of the prepared baking pan with a thin layer of sauce. Break the lasagna noodles to fit in a single layer in the bottom of the pan (see Note on page 112). Top with more of the sauce (enough to fully cover the pasta), half of the ricotta mixture, and one-third of the mozzarella. Repeat twice more, each time pressing down gently on the noodle layer to compress slightly before adding other ingredients. The final layer will be sauce and mozzarella. Sprinkle the top with the ¼ cup (25 g) Parmesan.

2 Spray a piece of foil with nonstick vegetable spray (without flour) and lay it, sprayed side down, loosely on top of the pan. Crimp the edges of the foil to keep the steam out of the pan.

Note: If you are using a push-pan instead of a springform, you will have fun. It is similar to a tart pan where the bottom is set into the pan. To remove the lasagna (or cheesecakes), place the pan onto a large can of tomatoes or similar heavy object. Then carefully press down on the sides of the pan, sliding it down and revealing the layers of the lasagna. When the sides are completely clear, lift the lasagna from its base and set on a cutting board before slicing into wedges and serving.

(continued)

Notes: The timing for the pasta may change depending on the brand of pasta you use. See page 98 for details.

Barilla lasagna noodles fit perfectly into a 7-inch (18 cm) round pan, but if you stack three sheets overlapping like the spokes of a wheel, they may not fully cook through in the center. Break them into smaller pieces and arrange in a jigsaw pattern, slightly overlapping.

3 Pour the water into the bottom of the inner pot. Place a trivet in the bottom. Using a sling, set the pan on the trivet. Close and lock the lid, making sure the steam release handle is in the sealing position. Cook on high pressure for 24 minutes. When it is finished, release the pressure naturally for 10 minutes, then turn the steam release handle to venting, releasing any remaining steam. Unlock the lid and open it carefully.

4 Lift the pan out of the pot, remove the foil, and check to see if it is done by inserting a knife in several places; it should meet no resistance. Set the pan on a baking sheet. If desired, place under the broiler to brown the cheese on top. Remove from the oven and set aside to rest for 10 minutes before cutting into servings, sprinkling a little chopped basil on top of each piece.

Tex-Mex Chili Mac

GLUTEN FREE • DAIRY-FREE OPTION •
SOY FREE • NUT FREE • EGG FREE

A favorite quick meal that we always had on hand were frozen entrées, but most of them are gluten full. This recipe is just as good and nearly as fast to make from scratch. It is great to be able to control all the ingredients and know exactly what you are serving your family. This recipe is full of flavor but not much heat. If you want a spicier version, add chipotle powder or a hot sauce (Sriracha brand is gluten free) to taste.

Yield About 4 servings

1 tablespoon (15 ml) olive or vegetable oil

½ onion, finely chopped

1 red bell pepper, stemmed, seeded, and finely chopped

1 pound (454 g) lean ground beef

2 cloves garlic, minced

2 tablespoons (16 g) gluten-free chili powder, such as Penzeys or McCormick brands

2 teaspoons (1 g) dried oregano

1 teaspoon ground cumin

2 cups (470 ml) beef stock (page 212)

½ cup (120 ml) tomato sauce

8 ounces (227 g) elbow macaroni, such as Barilla gluten-free brand

1½ cups (180 g) shredded cheese, such as cheddar or Colby

Chopped scallion, for garnish

1 Press Sauté on your electric pressure cooker and heat the oil in the inner pot. Add the onion and bell pepper, and cook until they begin to soften, about 3 minutes, stirring occasionally. Crumble the beef into the pot. Use a flat-edged wooden spatula to break up clumps as it cooks. When cooked through, stir in the garlic and cook for 30 seconds. Stir in the chili powder, oregano, and cumin.

2 Pour in the beef stock and tomato sauce. Add the pasta and do not stir but make sure the pasta pieces are submerged in the liquid. Press Cancel.

3 Close and lock the lid, making sure the steam release handle is in the sealing position. Cook on high pressure for 1 minute. When it is finished, release the pressure naturally for 4 minutes, then do a controlled release by holding the handle between the sealed and venting positions, releasing the remaining steam. When the float pin drops, unlock the lid and open it carefully. Press Cancel.

4 Stir the ingredients together in the pot. Sprinkle the cheese over the top, replace the lid, and let it rest for a couple minutes to melt the cheese. Scoop into bowls, sprinkle each with some of the scallions, and serve immediately.

Notes: Seasoning blends can hide gluten ingredients. Be diligent about checking labels and if all the ingredients aren't listed, contact the manufacturer to be sure they are safe to use. Penzeys and McCormick brands are both good at clearly labeling their products.

The timing for the pasta may change depending on the brand of pasta you use. See page 98 for details.

Vegetable Macaroni Salad

GLUTEN FREE • DAIRY FREE •
VEGETARIAN • NUT FREE

Pasta salad is standard fare all summer long, showing up on barbecue dinner tables everywhere. With the high-quality gluten-free pastas now available, you can make this easy salad and safely serve it to your entire family. Feel free to use any seasonal vegetables growing in your garden or that you find at your farmers' market to customize this salad.

Yield 6 to 8 servings

12 ounces (340 g) elbow macaroni, such as Barilla gluten-free brand

Olive or vegetable oil

2½ teaspoons (15 g) kosher or fine sea salt, divided

½ to ¾ cup (120 to 180 ml) gluten-free Italian salad dressing, such as Girard's Olde Venice Italian Dressing

1 teaspoon sugar (optional)

½ teaspoon freshly ground black pepper

½ teaspoon onion powder

¼ teaspoon ground celery seed

3 scallions, trimmed and finely chopped

2 stalks celery, trimmed and finely chopped

2 red bell peppers, cored, seeded, and finely chopped

1 large cucumber, finely chopped

½ pint (150 g) cherry tomatoes, cut in half

½ cup (50 g) sliced black olives (Lindsay brand is gluten-free)

3 tablespoons (9 g) chopped fresh parsley

1 Place the pasta in the inner pot of your electric pressure cooker. Add fresh water to cover the pasta by 1 inch (2.5 cm). Stir 2 teaspoons (12 g) of the salt into the water and make sure the pasta is not sticking to the bottom of the pot.

2 Close and lock the lid, with the steam release handle in the sealing position. Cook on high pressure for 1 minute. When it is finished, release the pressure naturally for 4 minutes, then turn the steam release handle to venting, releasing remaining steam. When the pressure valve drops, unlock the lid and open it carefully. Pour the pasta into a colander and rinse with cool water to stop the cooking, and then drain thoroughly. Transfer to a large mixing bowl.

3 In a bowl, whisk together the dressing, sugar (if using), ½ teaspoon salt, pepper, onion powder, and celery seed. Pour ½ cup (120 ml) over the pasta and stir in the vegetables and parsley, mixing until evenly distributed and everything is coated with the dressing. Taste and adjust the seasonings, adding more dressing if needed. Store in the refrigerator, covered, until ready to serve.

Note: The timing for the pasta may change depending on the brand of pasta you use. See page 98 for details.

6
MASTERFUL MAIN DISHES

Dinner is one less thing to worry about with your electric pressure cooker. Instead of having to plan ahead and use your oven for hours, you can toss everything in the pressure cooker. The range of dishes you can produce in one pot is simply amazing!

One place where electric pressure cookers really shine is with tough cuts of meat, which normally take hours and hours to become succulent. The technology makes short work of the tenderizing, cutting the time in half or more. The steaming and braising processes leave them luscious and moist without effort. Beef, chicken, fish, pork, ribs, and all types of proteins come out perfectly in your pressure cooker.

Cooking meat in a pressure cooker is wonderful, but who says meat has to be the center of a marvelous meal? Vegetables cooked in a pressure cooker come out just as fantastic. Pressure cooking brings out the natural flavors and delicious complexity of all types of vegetables. It is a fantastic tool for infusing herbs, spices, and other aromatics into your vegetables, legumes, and pulses, thereby creating flavorful, vegetable-focused main dishes. Don't believe us? Try our Vegetable Lasagna (page 118) or Lentil

Sloppy Joes (page 121)! These healthy main dishes are not only loaded with flavor, but they can also be on your table in about an hour. With these hearty and satisfying dishes, you'll find plenty of inspiration for your next Meatless Monday!

So whether you are looking for a way to impress guests or simply get a nutritious meal on the table after a long day at work, these are mouthwatering, delicious, gluten-free meals your whole family will enjoy!

Recipes

Vegetable Lasagna

GLUTEN FREE • VEGETARIAN • SOY FREE • NUT FREE

This vegetable lasagna is so hearty, you won't miss the meat. The layers of vegetables and noodles come together perfectly in the pressure cooker. It's stuffed with not only plenty of vegetables but also three different cheeses, so even your favorite meat-eaters are going to love it. Serve with a nice green salad and you've got a complete meal in under an hour! For a crisp top, put the finished lasagna under the broiler for a few minutes to brown. Be sure to watch it carefully so it doesn't burn.

Yield 4 servings

The pan you use for this recipe should be at least 3 inches (7.6 cm) deep. Anything less won't fit all the delicious vegetable and cheese layers.

1 tablespoon (15 ml) olive oil

1 medium onion, diced

4 cloves garlic, minced

1 teaspoon red pepper flakes

2 cups (140 g) sliced button mushrooms

1 cup (120 g) finely diced carrot

1 cup (150 g) finely diced red bell pepper

1½ cups (355 ml) water

1 cup (240 g) low-fat ricotta cheese or small-curd cottage cheese

1½ cups (180 g) part-skim mozzarella cheese, divided

1 cup (100 g) grated Parmesan cheese, divided

1 egg

1 tablespoon (6 g) dried oregano

1 teaspoon dried parsley

6 to 9 no-boil, oven-ready lasagna noodles, such as Barilla gluten-free brand

3 cups (750 g) your favorite gluten-free marinara sauce

¼ cup (10 g) chopped fresh basil leaves

2 medium zucchini, thinly sliced lengthwise

1 Press Sauté on your electric pressure cooker. When the inner pot is hot, add the oil and onion. Cook for 2 to 3 minutes, or until the onion begins to soften. Add the garlic and red pepper flakes and cook for an additional 30 seconds, until the garlic is fragrant.

2 Add the mushrooms, carrot, and bell pepper to the pot. Cook for another 2 minutes. Remove the sautéed vegetables to a medium bowl. Drain any excess liquids. Set aside.

3 Rinse your pot and dry well, inside and out. Return the inner pot to the body of your pressure cooker. Place a trivet in the bottom of the pot and add the water. Spray a 7 x 3-inch (18 x 7.6 cm) push pan or round cake pan with nonstick cooking spray.

4 In a small bowl, combine the ricotta cheese, 1 cup (120 g) of the mozzarella cheese, ½ cup (50 g) of the Parmesan cheese, egg, oregano, and parsley. Set aside.

(continued)

Notes: The timing for the pasta may change depending on the brand of pasta you use. See page 98 for details.

The Barilla lasagna noodles fit perfectly into a 7-inch (18 cm) round pan, but if you stack three sheets overlapping like the spokes of a wheel, they may not fully cook through in the center. Break them into smaller pieces and arrange in a jigsaw pattern, slightly overlapping.

5 Break 3 pasta pieces and arrange them evenly in the bottom of the pan. A little bit of overlap is fine. Spread 1 cup (250 g) of the marinara sauce over the noodles. Layer half of the chopped basil over the sauce. Add half of the zucchini slices and spread half of the drained vegetable mixture over the slices. Spread half of the cheese mixture over the vegetables, spreading as evenly as possible.

6 Repeat with another layer of pasta, sauce, basil, zucchini, vegetables, and cheese. Top with the remaining 3 pasta sheets and remaining 1 cup (250 g) tomato sauce. Sprinkle the remaining ½ cup (60 g) mozzarella and remaining ½ cup (50 g) Parmesan cheese on top.

7 Cover the pan with aluminum foil, crimping the edges to seal. Using a foil sling (see page 18), lower the lasagna pan onto the trivet.

8 Close and lock the lid, making sure the steam release knob is in the sealing position. Cook on high pressure for 20 minutes. When the cook time is finished, allow a 10-minute natural release, then turn the knob to the venting position, releasing any remaining steam. When the float pin drops, unlock the lid and open it carefully.

9 Allow the lasagna to sit for a few minutes to set, then carefully remove it from the pan.

Lentil Sloppy Joes

GLUTEN FREE • DAIRY FREE • NUT FREE • VEGETARIAN

When you need something hearty to feed a crowd, this is it! Grab a fork on the way, because these lentil sloppy Joes are definitely sloppy! Smoky, tender, slightly spicy, with a hint of sweetness and a rich tomato flavor, this recipe is quick to put together and sure to bring back memories of childhood dinners. Serve these with French fries or a green salad. If you want to skip the bread altogether, this mixture is great in lettuce cups or served over steamed rice.

Yield 4 servings

1 tablespoon (15 ml) vegetable oil

1 large yellow onion, diced

5 cloves garlic, minced

2 carrots, peeled and diced small

1 green bell pepper, cored, seeded, and diced

2 cups (380 g) brown or green lentils, rinsed

1 cup (235 ml) water or vegetable stock (page 214)

1 (14.5-ounce, or 406 g) can fire-roasted diced tomatoes (including juices)

1 (15-ounce, or 420 g) can tomato sauce

3 tablespoons (45 g) tomato paste

2 to 3 tablespoons (30 to 45 g) brown sugar (to taste)

2 tablespoons (30 ml) Worcestershire sauce (Lea & Perrins brand is gluten free)

2 teaspoons (4 g) ground cumin

1 tablespoon (6 g) chili powder

2 teaspoons (4 g) smoked paprika

4 gluten-free hamburger buns, such as Udi's, for serving

1 Press Sauté on your electric pressure cooker. When the inner pot is hot, add the oil. Add the onion and sauté until just beginning to soften, 3 minutes. Add the garlic and cook for an additional 30 seconds, until fragrant.

2 Add all the remaining ingredients (except the buns) to the pot and stir well.

3 Close and lock the lid, making sure the steam release knob is in the sealing position. Cook on high pressure for 15 minutes. When the cook time is finished, allow a full natural pressure release (about 20 minutes). When the float pin has dropped, unlock the lid and open it carefully.

4 Taste and adjust the seasonings as needed. Add more chili powder or cumin for spice and smokiness, brown sugar for a sweeter sloppy Joe, or a little more Worcestershire for deeper flavor.

Shrimp and Grits

GLUTEN FREE • NUT FREE • SOY FREE

This recipe is an easy way to impress guests or to serve as a quick weeknight dinner. It is so rich and decadent, yet it's still good old-fashioned, down-home casual fare. Add more hot sauce than is listed here if you like your grits with a bit more kick. Making the grits and the sauce together not only saves time but also frees you for other things, like setting the table or helping your kids with homework while dinner cooks.

Yield 4 servings

For the shrimp

1 pound (454 g) shrimp, peeled and deveined

1 tablespoon (3 g) Old Bay Seasoning (Old Bay is gluten free)

3 slices smoked bacon, diced (Applegate Farms has gluten-free bacon)

1 medium yellow onion, chopped

1 red or green bell pepper, cored, seeded, and chopped

3 cloves garlic, minced

½ cup (120 ml) chicken stock (page 213)

1 (14.5-ounce, or 406 g) can diced tomatoes

2 tablespoons (30 ml) freshly squeezed lemon juice

½ teaspoon Tabasco or hot sauce, to taste

½ teaspoon salt

½ teaspoon fresh cracked black pepper

¼ cup (60 ml) heavy cream

¼ cup (25 g) thinly sliced scallion, green parts only

For the grits

¾ cup (105 g) grits (such as Bob's Red Mill gluten-free coarse corn grits)

1½ cups (355 ml) whole milk

1½ cups (355 ml) water

½ teaspoon salt

½ teaspoon fresh cracked black pepper

2 tablespoons (28 g) unsalted butter

Shrimp

1 Pat the shrimp dry, sprinkle with the Old Bay Seasoning, and set aside.

2 Press Sauté on your electric pressure cooker. When the inner pot is hot, add the diced bacon and cook until crisp, 3 to 5 minutes. Transfer the bacon to a paper towel–lined plate, but leave the bacon drippings in the pot. Add the onion and bell pepper to the pot and cook until the onion is soft and translucent, 2 to 3 minutes. Add the garlic and cook for an additional 30 seconds, until fragrant.

3 Add the chicken stock to the pot, stirring well to release any browned bits from the bottom. Add the tomatoes and their juices, lemon juice, hot sauce, salt, and pepper. Stir to combine. Press Cancel.

4 Place a trivet in the pot. Make sure the base of the trivet sits above the sauce.

Grits

1 In a medium glass or stainless steel bowl that will fit inside your pressure cooker, whisk together the grits, milk, water, salt, and pepper. Cover the bowl with aluminum foil, crimping the edges to seal. Using a foil sling (see page 18), carefully place the bowl on the trivet inside the inner pot.

2 Close and lock the lid, making sure the steam release handle is in the sealing position. Cook on high pressure for 10 minutes. Allow a natural pressure release for 15 minutes, then turn the knob to the venting position, releasing any remaining steam. When the float pin drops, unlock the lid and open it carefully. Remove the bowl with the grits and set aside.

3 Remove the trivet from the pot using a pair of tongs. Add the seasoned shrimp to the pot. Close and lock the lid again to allow the shrimp to finish cooking in the residual heat, 6 to 8 minutes.

4 While the shrimp are cooking, add the butter to the grits and whisk until the butter is completely melted and the mixture is creamy.

5 Open the pressure cooker and gently stir the shrimp. Press Cancel. Press Sauté, then stir the cream into the shrimp mixture. Heat until warmed through, stirring constantly. Do not boil the sauce.

6 Spoon the grits into individual serving dishes, then top with the shrimp and sauce. Garnish with the scallions and reserved bacon.

Steamed Salmon and Garlic Red Potatoes

GLUTEN FREE • NUT FREE • SOY FREE • EGG FREE

This is a complete one-pot dinner! It's simple to put together and easy enough for a midweek meal. The steamed salmon is flaky and the fish really shines with the simple seasonings of salt, pepper, and lemon. Steaming the onions and potatoes with the salmon and adding the spinach at the end means not only a well-rounded and healthy dinner but also only one pan to wash afterward.

Yield 4 servings

4 tablespoons (56 g) unsalted butter, divided

1 cup (235 ml) chicken stock (page 213)

1 pound (454 g) small red-skinned potatoes, quartered

1 large onion, cut into 8 wedges

1 teaspoon salt, divided

1 teaspoon freshly ground black pepper, divided

4 (5- to 6-ounce, or 140 to 168 g, each) skin-on center-cut salmon fillets (¾ to 1 inch, or 1.8 to 2.5 cm, thick)

1 teaspoon grated lemon zest

2 tablespoons (20 g) minced garlic

3 cups (105 g) baby spinach

1 tablespoon (2 g) fresh thyme leaves

1 tablespoon (2 g) fresh rosemary leaves, minced

Lemon wedges, for serving

1 Press Sauté on your electric pressure cooker. When the inner pot is hot, add 3 table-spoons (42 g) of the butter. Once the butter has melted, press Cancel.

2 Pour the chicken stock into the pot with the butter. Add the potatoes and onion wedges. Sprinkle ½ teaspoon each of the salt and pepper over the vegetables. Place a long-legged trivet over the potatoes and onions. Place an expandable steamer basket on top of the trivet.

3 Season the salmon fillets generously with the lemon zest and remaining ½ teaspoon each salt and pepper. Place skin side down on the steamer basket.

4 Close and lock the lid, making sure the steam release handle is in the sealing position. Cook on high pressure for 3 minutes. When the cook time is finished, do a quick pressure release by carefully moving the sealing handle to venting and allowing all the steam to escape. When the float pin drops, unlock the lid and open it carefully. Press Cancel.

5 Remove the salmon and place on a serving tray; tent lightly with foil to keep warm. Remove the steamer basket and trivet. Drain the potatoes and onions, reserving ¼ cup (60 ml) of the cooking liquid. Return the vegetables to the pot, along with the reserved cooking liquid.

6 Press Sauté. When the potatoes start sizzling, add the garlic and cook, stirring, until softened, 1 to 2 minutes; stir in the remaining 1 tablespoon (14 g) butter and additional salt and pepper if desired.

7 Press Cancel. Add the spinach, thyme, and rosemary to the potatoes and stir until the greens are wilted.

8 Divide the potato/spinach mixture equally among 4 plates. Top the greens with the salmon and serve with lemon wedges.

Use salmon with the skin attached. It will help hold the fillet together as it cooks.

Roast Turkey Breast with Easy Gravy

GLUTEN FREE • SOY FREE • NUT FREE
• EGG FREE

This easy roast turkey can be on your dinner table in just over an hour. As the turkey cooks, it's creating the base for a flavorful gravy that comes together quickly without any flour, making it a completely gluten-free meal. This meal is fancy enough to serve for the holidays or a special Sunday dinner, but it is also easy enough to make during the week if you're in the mood for some solid comfort food. Searing the turkey before you cook it will give it a nice golden brown color and a deeper flavor! Serve with Mashed Potatoes (page 183).

Yield 8 servings

For the turkey

3 tablespoons (45 ml) olive or vegetable oil, divided

1 (4- to 5-pound, or 1.8 to 2.3 kg) turkey breast (Jenni-O brand is gluten free)

3 tablespoons (6 g) chopped fresh thyme

2 tablespoons (6 g) chopped fresh rosemary

2 teaspoons (12 g) salt

1 tablespoon (6 g) freshly cracked black pepper

5 cloves garlic, minced

2 tablespoons (28 g) unsalted butter

½ medium onion, sliced

1 cup (235 ml) chicken stock (page 213)

For the gravy

3 tablespoons (42 g) unsalted butter

3 tablespoons (24 g) cornstarch or potato starch

½ cup (120 ml) half-and-half

Salt and pepper to taste

Turkey

1 Drizzle 1 tablespoon (15 ml) of the oil all over the turkey breast. Coat the breast with the thyme, rosemary, salt, pepper, and minced garlic.

2 Press Sauté on your electric pressure cooker. When the inner pot is hot, add the 2 tablespoons (28 g) butter and the remaining 2 tablespoons (30 ml) olive oil. When the butter is melted, add the turkey breast and sear on all sides. This should take about 8 minutes. When the turkey is a nice golden brown, transfer to a plate or a cutting board.

3 In the remaining turkey fat, add the onion and sauté until just beginning to soften, 3 to 4 minutes. Press Cancel.

4 Add the stock to the bottom of the pot. Stir to scrape up any browned bits. Place the trivet in the bottom of the inner pot, on top of the onions. Place the browned turkey on top of the trivet.

5 Close and lock the lid, making sure the steam release knob is in the sealing position. Cook on high pressure for 35 minutes. When the turkey is finished cooking, allow a 15-minute natural release, then move the handle to venting and release any remaining steam. When the float pin drops, unlock the lid and open it carefully.

6 Check your turkey with an instant-read thermometer to ensure it is at least 165°F (74°C). If it's not 165°F (74°C), return the lid and cook at high pressure for an additional 4 to 5 minutes with a 10-minute natural release. Once your turkey is at a safe 165°F (74°C), remove it from your pressure cooker and transfer it to a cutting board. Cover the turkey breast completely with aluminum foil and let it rest for at least 15 minutes before slicing.

Gravy

1 After removing the turkey breast from the pressure cooker, return your pressure cooker to the Sauté or Browning setting. Add the 3 tablespoons (42 g) butter to the liquid at the bottom of the pan. Cook until the butter is melted.

2 In a small bowl, whisk together the cornstarch and 3 tablespoons (45 ml) of the cooking liquid from the pot to form a slurry. Add the slurry back to the pot and continue to whisk until the gravy thickens, about 2 minutes. Add the half-and-half and stir until just heated through. Add salt and pepper to taste.

3 Pour the gravy over the sliced turkey breast and serve.

If you're a fan of crispier skin, place your cooked turkey on a sheet pan under the broiler for about 5 minutes while you're making the gravy. Watch it carefully so it doesn't get too brown.

Classic Whole Baked Chicken

GLUTEN FREE • DAIRY FREE • SOY FREE • EGG FREE • NUT FREE

This whole baked chicken will make a meal in itself, but you can also cook it on its own and use the meat for any number of other dishes. Try it with our Millet and Chicken Greek Salad (page 93). Be sure to save the chicken carcass to make your own chicken stock (page 213). Serve this chicken as part of a complete meal, with Mashed Potatoes (page 183) or Cheesy Au Gratin Potatoes (page 184).

Yield 4 servings

Make sure your chicken fits easily inside the inner pot of your pressure cooker. Some whole chickens might be too large.

1 (3- to 5-pound, or 1362 to 2270 g) whole chicken

1 tablespoon (18 g) salt, divided

1 lemon, cut in half

1 onion, cut into quarters

2 teaspoons (4 g) freshly ground pepper

2 teaspoons (4 g) paprika

1 teaspoon dried thyme

1 cup (235 ml) water

Oil or melted unsalted butter (optional, for crisping skin)

1 Remove any giblets or other innards from the cavity of the chicken. Pat dry with a paper towel. Sprinkle 1 teaspoon (6 g) of the salt inside the chicken. Place the cut lemon and onion pieces inside the chicken cavity. Sprinkle the remaining 2 teaspoons (12 g) salt, pepper, paprika, and thyme evenly over the chicken.

2 Put a trivet in the inner pot of your electric pressure cooker and add the water. Place the seasoned chicken, with the breast facing up, on top of the trivet.

3 Close and lock the lid, making sure the steam release knob is in the sealing position. Cook on high pressure for 6 minutes per pound (454 g).

3-pound (1.4 kg) chicken = 18 minutes

4-pound (1.8 kg) chicken = 24 minutes

5-pound (2.3 kg) chicken = 30 minutes

If your chicken is between weights, add 3 minutes for every half pound (227 g). Example: One 4½-pound (2 kg) chicken would equal 27 minutes on high pressure.

4 When the cooking time is finished, allow a natural release for 20 minutes, then move the pressure release knob to the venting position and release any remaining steam. When the float pin drops, unlock the lid and open it carefully.

5 If you like your chicken skin crispy, after removing it from the pot, transfer to a foil-lined baking sheet. Brush with oil or melted butter and place under the broiler for 2 to 4 minutes.

Arroz con Pollo

GLUTEN FREE • SOY FREE • NUT FREE • DAIRY FREE

Arroz con pollo is a perfect all-in-one meal. The chicken, rice, and vegetables simmer together, enhancing each other and giving the cook a break. Using juicy dark meat chicken thighs is the key to the rich flavoring of this easy dish.

Yield 6 servings

Note: Dicing all the vegetables in the morning, or the night before you make this dish, will make it much quicker to come together!

2 pounds (908 g) boneless, skinless chicken thighs, cut into quarters

2 teaspoons (12 g) salt

2 teaspoons (6 g) pepper

2 tablespoons (20 g) minced garlic

3 tablespoons (45 ml) vegetable oil

1 red bell pepper, cored and diced

1 green bell pepper, cored and diced

1 medium onion, diced

2¼ cups (530 ml) chicken stock (page 213), divided

2 teaspoons (6 g) ground cumin

1½ teaspoons dried oregano

1½ cups (360 g) canned diced tomatoes

½ cup (120 ml) tomato sauce

1½ cups (270 g) uncooked long-grain white rice

2 tablespoons (2 g) chopped fresh cilantro, for garnish

1 Rub the chicken thighs all over with the salt, pepper, and garlic.

2 Press Sauté on your electric pressure cooker. When the inner pot is hot, add the oil. When the oil is hot, add the chicken pieces and brown for 3 minutes on each side, stirring occasionally. Remove the chicken to a plate.

3 Add the bell peppers and onion to the pot and sauté for 3 minutes, or until the vegetables just begin to soften.

4 Add 1 cup (235 ml) of the chicken stock to the pot. Use a wooden spatula to gently deglaze the pan, scraping up any flavorful browned bits that have stuck to the bottom. Add the remaining 1¼ cups (295 ml) stock, cumin, oregano, tomatoes, tomato sauce, and rice to the pot. Stir well. Press Cancel.

5 Return the chicken to the pot and submerge in the sauce with the rice.

6 Close and lock the lid, making sure the steam release handle is in the sealing position. Cook on high pressure for 20 minutes. When the cook time is finished, allow a 10-minute natural release, then do a quick release to vent any remaining steam. When the float pin drops, unlock the lid and open it carefully.

7 Divide the rice equally among serving dishes and top with the chicken. Serve with a garnish of chopped, fresh cilantro.

Chicken Pot Pie Casserole

GLUTEN FREE • SOY FREE • NUT FREE

While this pot pie may not have a traditional crust on top, the addition of gluten-free linguini noodles makes it a hearty casserole that will remind you of the oven-baked version, done in far less time! You can get as creative as you like with this recipe, too. Use any frozen vegetable combination you prefer, or you can use fresh vegetables. If you use fresh vegetables, dice them into small, uniform pieces so they will cook evenly. Serve with a salad for a complete meal.

Yield 8 servings

Note: The timing for the pasta may change depending on the brand of pasta you use. See page 98 for details.

2 tablespoons (30 ml) vegetable oil

1½ pounds (680 g) boneless, skinless chicken breasts, cut into bite-size cubes

1 teaspoon salt

2 teaspoons (6 g) pepper

1 medium onion, diced

1 tablespoon (10 g) minced garlic

1 cup (150 g) frozen peas and carrots

½ cup (75 g) frozen green beans

½ cup (75 g) frozen corn kernels

12 ounces (340 g) linguini noodles, such as Barilla gluten-free brand, broken in half

3¼ cups (765 ml) chicken stock (page 213)

2 tablespoons (4 g) fresh thyme leaves

¾ cup (180 ml) heavy cream

1 Press Sauté on your electric pressure cooker. When the inner pot is hot, add the oil. Generously season the chicken pieces with the salt and pepper. Add to the oil. Sauté for 2 to 3 minutes per side until the outside of the chicken is white. Remove the chicken from the pan.

2 Add the onion to the pan and sauté until soft but not brown, 2 to 3 minutes. Add the garlic and cook an additional 30 seconds, until fragrant. Press Cancel.

3 Return the chicken to the pot and add the frozen vegetables, linguini noodles, chicken stock, and thyme.

4 Close and lock the lid, making sure the steam release handle is in the sealing position. Press Manual and cook on high pressure for 6 minutes.

5 When the cook time is finished, do a quick pressure release and allow all the steam to escape. When the float pin drops, unlock the lid and open it carefully. Press Cancel.

6 Stir in the heavy cream. Press Sauté. Allow the mixture to cook for another 2 to 3 minutes, or until it thickens to your desired consistency.

Classic Coq au Vin

GLUTEN FREE • SOY FREE • NUT FREE • EGG FREE

This classic French stew combines red wine, mushrooms, carrots, and braised chicken thighs, topped with crunchy bits of bacon. We are so thankful for companies like Applewood Farms for giving us gluten-free bacon, making this dish possible. While you could make it without the bacon, it does give a bit of extra salt and texture to the stew that just can't be beat. Serve this stew in big bowls with toasted bread, or make it extra indulgent and serve it over our Mashed Potatoes (page 183).

Yield 8 servings

2 tablespoons (30 ml) vegetable oil, divided

6 strips gluten-free bacon, diced (Applewood Farms is gluten free)

2 teaspoons (12 g) salt

1½ teaspoons freshly cracked black pepper

3 pounds (1362 g) boneless, skinless chicken thighs

1 cup (150 g) pearl onions, blanched and peeled (you can use frozen)

2 tablespoons (20 g) minced garlic

1 tablespoon (14 g) unsalted butter

1 (12-ounce, or 340 g) package white mushrooms, quartered

1½ cups (355 ml) gluten-free red wine, divided (see Note, opposite)

1 cup (235 ml) chicken stock (page 213)

3 tablespoons (45 g) tomato paste

3 sprigs fresh thyme

1 teaspoon oregano leaves

1½ cups (180 g) baby carrots

2 tablespoons (16 g) cornstarch

2 tablespoons (30 ml) cold water

3 tablespoons (12 g) chopped flat-leaf parsley, for garnish

1 Press Sauté on your electric pressure cooker. When the inner pot is hot, add 1 tablespoon (15 ml) of the oil and the diced bacon. Brown the bacon until crisp, stirring frequently. Remove to a paper towel–lined plate. Leave the bacon fat in the pot.

2 Sprinkle the salt and pepper over the chicken thighs. Add the chicken to the bacon fat in the pot and brown on both sides, 5 to 6 minutes per side. Remove the chicken to a serving platter, leaving the fat in the pan.

3 Add the onions and cook, stirring frequently, until softened and lightly caramelized. Add the garlic and cook an additional 30 seconds, until fragrant. Remove the onions and garlic to the platter with the chicken.

4 Add the remaining 1 tablespoon (15 ml) oil and the butter to the pot. When the butter is melted, add the mushrooms and cook until golden. Season with salt and pepper. Remove to a small bowl and cover with foil. Set aside.

5 Add 1 cup (235 ml) of the wine to deglaze the pot and let it almost completely evaporate to concentrate the flavor and remove most of the liquid. Press Cancel.

6 Stir in the remaining ½ cup (120 ml) wine, chicken stock, tomato paste, thyme, oregano, and carrots.

7 Add the onions, garlic, and browned chicken back to the pot, along with any juices that may have collected. Close and lock the lid, making sure the steam release handle is in the sealing position. Cook on high pressure for 12 minutes.

8 When the cook time is finished, do a quick pressure release and allow all the steam to escape. When the float pin drops, unlock the lid and open it carefully. Use a slotted spoon to remove the chicken from the pressure cooker to a serving dish.

9 Combine the cornstarch and water in a small bowl, whisking until smooth. Add the cornstarch mixture to the sauce in the pot, stirring constantly. Press Sauté and bring the sauce to a boil, stirring constantly. Allow the sauce to simmer until it thickens, about 2 minutes. Add the mushrooms back to the pot and stir, coating them well with the sauce.

10 Pour the sauce over the chicken. Sprinkle with the crumbled bacon and chopped parsley.

Note: Although wine is considered gluten free, to be super careful for highly reactive people, look for winemakers that use only stainless steel tanks for aging their wines. There is a very rare possibility of contamination from casks that are sealed with gluten-containing ingredients.

Chicken Tikka Masala

GLUTEN FREE • SOY FREE • NUT FREE

Achieving the traditional Indian flavor of this dish means it does take a few extra steps, but it is worth it once you taste it! The turmeric adds a vibrant color and the addition of extra garam masala at the end not only enhances the aroma of the masala sauce, but it also allows those warm Indian flavors of cumin and coriander to come shining through. Cooking the rice in the pot along with the chicken and savory sauce means you can have a complete dinner on the table in under an hour.

Yield 4 servings

For the sauce

1 teaspoon ground coriander

2 teaspoons (6 g) ground cumin

¼ teaspoon ground cardamom

1 teaspoon turmeric

1 teaspoon kosher salt

½ teaspoon freshly ground black pepper

¼ teaspoon cayenne pepper

1½ teaspoons smoked paprika

1 tablespoon (8 g) garam masala (Penzeys brand is gluten free)

1 tablespoon (8 g) grated peeled fresh ginger (from a 1-inch, or 2.5 cm, piece)

1½ cups (360 g) canned tomato puree

3 tablespoons (45 g) tomato paste

½ cup (120 ml) chicken stock (page 213)

For the chicken

2 tablespoons (30 ml) olive oil

1½ pounds (680 g) boneless, skinless chicken thighs, cut into bite-size pieces

1 large onion, thinly sliced

½ cup (120 ml) chicken stock (page 213)

For the rice

2 cups (348 g) jasmine rice (Lundberg Farms brand is gluten free)

1 tablespoon (14 g) unsalted butter

2¼ cups (530 ml) water

For finishing

2 teaspoons (6 g) garam masala (Penzeys brand is gluten free)

½ cup (120 ml) heavy cream

½ cup (8 g) chopped fresh cilantro, for garnish

Sauce

1 In a medium bowl, combine all the ingredients for the sauce. Set aside.

Chicken

1 Press Sauté on your electric pressure cooker. When the inner pot is hot, add the oil and brown the chicken pieces for 2 to 3 minutes per side. Remove the chicken to a plate when brown. You may need to do this in batches.

2 Add the onion to the pot and sauté for 3 minutes, until slightly soft. Pour in the chicken stock, scraping with a wooden spoon to get up any browned bits on the bottom of the pot. Press Cancel.

3 Pour the prepared sauce into the pot and stir to combine. Return the chicken to the pot and fully submerge in the sauce. Add a long-legged trivet to the pot over the chicken and sauce, making sure the legs of the trivet are touching the bottom of the pot.

Rice

1 Place the rice in a fine-mesh colander and rinse under cold water until the water runs clear, about 1 minute. Place the rinsed rice, butter, and water into a 7 x 3-inch (18 x 7.6 cm) cake pan. Cover the pan with foil, crimping well to seal the edges. Lower the rice pan on top of the trivet using a foil sling (see page 18).

2 Close and lock the lid, making sure the steam release handle is in the sealing position. Cook on high pressure for 15 minutes. When the cook time is finished, do a quick pressure release by carefully moving the sealing handle to venting and allowing all the steam to escape. When the float pin drops, unlock the lid and open it carefully. Press Cancel.

Finishing

1 Remove the rice pan from the cooking pot and set aside. Press Sauté. Add the garam masala to the liquid in the pot and simmer for 10 minutes to thicken, stirring often. Add the heavy cream and heat through, 2 more minutes.

2 Serve the chicken in big bowls with the rice and masala sauce, garnished with cilantro.

If you don't like cilantro, substitute flat-leaf parsley or chopped scallion.

Chicken Burrito Bowls

GLUTEN FREE • SOY FREE • NUT FREE

Loaded with rice, beans, and hearty seasonings, these chicken burrito bowls are fun for a family movie night or for a crowd. Assemble all your favorite toppings on the side and allow everyone to choose their favorites. Because this makes such big portions, it's also great for meal prep! Divide this up for lunches during the week and you're all set.

Yield 6 servings

1 tablespoon (8 g) chili powder

2 teaspoons (6 g) ground cumin

2 teaspoons (4 g) ground oregano

¼ teaspoon cayenne pepper

1 teaspoon salt

1 teaspoon black pepper

1 pound (454 g) chicken breasts, diced into 1-inch (2.5 cm) cubes

2 tablespoons (30 ml) vegetable oil

1 large onion, diced

2 teaspoons (7 g) minced garlic

1 (16-ounce, or 454 g) can black beans, rinsed and drained

1 cup (235 ml) chicken stock (page 213)

1 (16-ounce, or 454 g) can diced tomatoes, drained

1 cup (235 g) fresh salsa

1 cup (180 g) uncooked long-grain white rice (not instant)

¼ cup (4 g) chopped fresh cilantro

1 green bell pepper, cored and diced

½ cup (75 g) crumbled cotija cheese, for serving

½ cup (50 g) thinly sliced scallion, for serving

1 cup (230 g) sour cream, for serving

1 large avocado, peeled, pitted, and diced, for serving

1 In a small bowl, whisk together chili powder, cumin, oregano, cayenne, salt, and pepper. Generously season the chicken with the spice mixture. Reserve any unused spice blend for another dish.

2 Press Sauté on your pressure cooker. When the inner pot is hot, add the oil. Add the chicken pieces and sauté until golden brown, 3 to 4 minutes per side. Remove to a paper towel–lined plate.

3 Add the onion to the pot and sauté until soft, 2 to 3 minutes. Add the garlic and cook an additional 30 seconds, until fragrant. Press Cancel.

4 Return the chicken to the pot with the onions and garlic. Add the black beans, chicken stock, tomatoes, salsa, and rice. Be sure to add the rice last, placing it on top of everything else so the rice doesn't burn.

Gently press the rice down into the sauce, so it is completely submerged, but don't stir.

5 Close and lock the lid, making sure the steam release handle is in the sealing position. Cook on high pressure for 8 minutes. When the cook time is finished, allow a 5-minute natural pressure release, then do a quick pressure release. When the float pin drops, unlock the lid and open it carefully.

6 Add the cilantro and bell pepper to the pot. Close the lid again and allow the bell pepper to steam in the residual heat for 3 to 4 minutes.

7 Press Cancel. Remove the lid and stir well. Divide the mixture evenly among 6 bowls. Top with the cheese, scallions, sour cream, and avocados, or use any of your favorite burrito toppings!

Southwestern Meatloaf

DAIRY FREE • SOY FREE • NUT FREE • EGG FREE

Most meatloaf recipes have eggs and bread crumbs in them as binders. I have found that you don't need either. The loaf will hold together without the binders, and that gives us a gluten-free dinner! By sautéing the vegetables, they soften enough to easily be mixed into the ground meat. Just be sure to chop them finely or it will be harder to make the loaf hold together. Loaded with the flavors of the American Southwest, this is not your mother's meatloaf. Serve with Mashed Potatoes (page 183), if you like.

Yield 4 servings

If you have picky eaters who won't touch vegetables, you can puree them with a little water or tomato sauce after cooking and mix the puree into the meat. They will eat their vegetables without ever knowing it!

To brown the top of the meatloaf, slide it under the broiler for a few minutes, once it's on the baking sheet.

1 tablespoon (15 ml) olive or vegetable oil

½ large onion, very finely chopped

2 stalks celery, very finely chopped

2 carrots, very finely chopped

1 red bell pepper, cored, seeded, and very finely chopped

1 pound (454 g) lean ground beef

1 tablespoon (15 ml) Worcestershire sauce

2 teaspoons (1 g) chopped fresh cilantro

2 teaspoons (4 g) gluten-free ancho chile powder or chili powder

1 teaspoon kosher or fine sea salt

1 teaspoon ground cumin

½ teaspoon freshly ground black pepper

¼ teaspoon garlic powder (*not* garlic salt)

¼ cup (60 ml) barbecue sauce

1 cup (60 ml) water for the bottom of the pot

1 Press Sauté on your electric pressure cooker. When the inner pot is hot, add the oil. Add the onion, celery, carrots, and pepper and cook, stirring often, until the onion has softened, 3 to 5 minutes. Press Cancel. Remove the inner pot from the machine and set aside to cool slightly.

2 In a bowl, combine the meat with the Worcestershire and seasonings until evenly coated. Fold in the cooled vegetables. When evenly distributed, pat the meat into a mounded disk about 6 inches (15 cm) in diameter and place in a 7-inch (18 cm) round baking pan. Brush the barbecue sauce over the top of the loaf. Cover the pan with foil. Wipe out the inner pot.

3 Place a trivet in the bottom of the inner pot and pour in the water. Set the meatloaf onto a rack with handles or a foil sling (see page 18) and lower onto the trivet. Close and lock the lid, making sure the steam release handle is in the sealing position. Cook on high pressure for 22 minutes, or until an instant-read thermometer registers at least 160°F (71°C) when inserted into the center of the meatloaf.

4 When it is finished, release the pressure naturally for 8 minutes, then release the rest of the pressure by moving the handle to the venting position. Unlock the lid and open it carefully.

5 Lift the sling out of the inner pot, carefully remove the foil from the pan, and transfer the meatloaf to a baking sheet.

6 Cut into slices to serve and pass additional barbecue sauce at the table.

Marvelous Meatball Stroganoff

GLUTEN FREE • NUT FREE

This dish has a kid-friendly twist by using turkey meatballs instead of flank steak. The meatballs are a fun and different addition and don't require any flour or bread crumbs as a binder. In a healthy twist, it doesn't use canned soup to achieve the traditional deep, rich flavor, bypassing an ingredient that usually has gluten in it. Serve over Mashed Potatoes (page 183) or your favorite gluten-free noodles.

Yield 5 servings (4 meatballs each)

1½ pounds (681 g) ground turkey (Jennie-O brand is gluten-free)

1 egg

1 tablespoon (15 ml) milk

2 teaspoons (5 g) onion powder

¼ cup (12 g) chopped fresh parsley, plus more for garnish

2 tablespoons (4 g) fresh thyme leaves

1 teaspoon salt

2 teaspoons (4 g) freshly ground black pepper

2 tablespoons (30 ml) olive oil

1 medium onion, thinly sliced

3 cloves garlic, minced

2½ cups (588 ml) beef stock (page 212), divided

½ cup (120 g) sour cream

2 teaspoons (5 g) smoked paprika

1 tablespoon (15 g) tomato paste

1 tablespoon (6 g) beef bouillon granules (Herb-Ox brand is gluten free)

½ teaspoon Worcestershire sauce (Lee & Perrins brand is gluten free)

½ pound (227 g) sliced button mushrooms

2 tablespoons (16 g) cornstarch

2 tablespoons (30 ml) cold water

1 In a large bowl, combine the ground turkey, egg, milk, onion powder, parsley, thyme, salt, and pepper until just combined. Shape into 20 (1-inch, or 2.5 cm) meatballs.

2 Press Sauté on your electric pressure cooker. When the inner pot is hot, add the oil and brown the meatballs, 2 to 3 minutes per side. Once the meatballs are brown, transfer them to a serving dish and set aside.

3 Add the sliced onion to the pot and cook until just tender, 3 to 4 minutes. Add the garlic and cook for an additional 30 seconds, until fragrant. Add 1 cup (235 ml) of the beef stock to the pan and scrape up any browned bits on the bottom of the pot.

4 In a small bowl, combine the remaining 1½ cups (355 ml) beef stock, sour cream, paprika, tomato paste, bouillon, and Worcestershire sauce. Stir until well combined. Add to the onion mixture already in the pan. Return the meatballs to the pot, submerging them completely in the sauce.

5 Close and lock the lid, making sure the steam release handle is in the sealing position. Cook on high pressure for 10 minutes. When the cooking time is finished, turn off your pressure cooker and allow a natural release of 20 minutes, or until the float pin drops. When the float pin has dropped, unlock the lid and open it carefully.

6 Add the sliced mushrooms to the pot. Stir well, then close the lid and let sit for 3 minutes to soften the mushrooms.

7 In a small bowl, mix the cornstarch and cold water together to create a slurry. Press Sauté or Browning on your electric pressure cooker again and allow the sauce to heat up. When the sauce is bubbling, add the cornstarch mixture to the pot and whisk constantly for 2 minutes, or until the sauce thickens.

8 Sprinkle with additional parsley, if desired.

Note: If you are a fan of mushrooms, feel free to add in a few extra! The richness of the mushrooms adds a great depth of flavor.

Beef Short Ribs and Mushrooms with Red Wine Sauce

GLUTEN FREE • DAIRY FREE • NUT FREE • SOY FREE

When the wind is blowing and you are bundled in heavy sweaters, you want warm, rich, and filling comfort foods. These short ribs will satisfy your deepest cravings and fill every tummy. Serve these over Mashed Potatoes (page 183) or Savory Creamy Polenta (page 87) so you can enjoy every drop of the succulent sauce!

Yield 3 to 4 servings

2 tablespoons (30 ml) olive or vegetable oil

3 pounds (1362 g) bone-in beef short ribs, cut into smaller pieces

1 medium onion, chopped

2 carrots, chopped

2 stalks celery, chopped

1 large bell pepper, cored and chopped

2 poblano peppers, chopped

½ cup (120 ml) gluten-free dry red wine (see Note, page 133)

1 cup (235 ml) beef stock (page 212)

2 tablespoons (30 ml) balsamic vinegar

2 tablespoons (30 g) tomato paste

5 sprigs fresh or 4 teaspoons (2 g) dried thyme

2 sprigs fresh or 2 teaspoons (1 g) dried rosemary

2 bay leaves

Kosher or fine sea salt and freshly ground black pepper, to taste

2 tablespoons (30 ml) cool water

1 tablespoon (8 g) cornstarch or 1½ tablespoons (12 g) potato starch (*not* potato flour)

8 ounces (227 g) small white or cremini mushrooms, cleaned and quartered

1 Press Sauté on your electric pressure cooker. Pour the oil into the inner pot. When the oil is hot, add half the ribs and brown well on both sides. Transfer to a platter and repeat with the remaining ribs. Add the vegetables to the pot and cook, stirring often, until the onions are translucent, about 5 minutes.

2 In a large measuring cup, stir together the wine, beef stock, balsamic vinegar, and tomato paste. When the paste is dissolved, pour the mixture into the pot and scrape the bottom. Stir in the herbs and seasonings. Press Cancel. Return the ribs to the pot.

3 Close and lock the lid, making sure the steam release handle is in the sealing position before cooking on high pressure for 35 to 40 minutes, depending on rib size. When the time is up, let the pressure naturally release for 15 minutes, then turn the steam release handle to venting and release any remaining steam. Press Cancel. Unlock the lid and open it carefully.

4 Transfer the ribs to a clean platter. Pour the cooking liquid through a fat separator, straining out the solids, and pour the juices back into the pot, leaving the fat behind. Press Sauté and bring the liquid to a boil. Cook, whisking often, for about 5 minutes to reduce the sauce.

5 In a small bowl, whisk together the water and cornstarch until smooth. Stir the resulting slurry into the sauce, whisking constantly, until thickened. Taste and adjust the seasonings with salt and pepper. Press Cancel.

6 Return ribs to the sauce. Stir in the mushrooms, replace the lid, and let sit for 5 to 8 minutes. Serve the ribs drizzled with the sauce.

Ropa Vieja (Cuban Beef Stew)

GLUTEN FREE • DAIRY FREE • SOY FREE • NUT FREE • EGG FREE

Ropa vieja, loosely translated as "old clothes," is one of the quintessential Cuban foods, their interpretation of beef stew, that is also found throughout the Caribbean. The seasonings, peppers, and olives make it exotic and enticing. Prepare it a day ahead to give the flavors time to fully develop and you'll have a delicious dinner in a snap. Give it a try and you will be amazed how quickly tough beef becomes packed with tantalizing flavor and fall-apart tender!

Yield 4 to 6 servings

For the stew

2 tablespoons (30 ml) olive or vegetable oil

2½ pounds (1135 g) chuck roast, cut into 3-inch (7.5 cm) chunks (discard large pieces of fat)

1 large onion, chopped

2 red bell peppers, cored and chopped

4 Cubanelle or Anaheim peppers, seeded and chopped

1 tablespoon (8 g) paprika

1 tablespoon (2 g) dried oregano

2 teaspoons (6 g) ground cumin

2 teaspoons (12 g) kosher or fine sea salt

1 teaspoon freshly ground black pepper

1 teaspoon smoked paprika

½ teaspoon ground allspice

3 cloves garlic, minced

½ cup (120 ml) gluten-free dry white wine (see Note, page 133)

1 cup (235 ml) beef stock (page 212) or chicken stock (page 213)

1 (15-ounce, or 420 g) can diced tomatoes (with their juice)

2 bay leaves

½ cup (75 g) golden raisins or dried currants

½ cup (50 g) green olives, preferably pimiento-stuffed Spanish olives, sliced

1 teaspoon apple cider vinegar

For serving

Cooked white rice (page 82)

Chopped fresh cilantro or parsley

Black beans, optional (see Note, page 142)

Stew

1 Press Sauté on your pressure cooker. Add the oil to the inner pot and, when hot, brown the meat on both sides. Transfer to a plate and set aside. Add the onion and peppers and cook, stirring often, until slightly softened, about 5 minutes. Sprinkle on the paprika, oregano, cumin, salt, pepper, smoked paprika, and allspice, stirring to evenly coat the vegetables. Add the garlic and cook for 30 seconds. Add the wine and deglaze the pan by scraping any browned bits off the bottom of the pot. Stir in the stock and tomatoes.

(continued)

Notes: If you want a thicker sauce, you can use a cornstarch slurry. Whisk 1 or 2 tablespoons (8 to 16 g) cornstarch into ¼ cup (60 ml) cool water. Transfer the meat to a platter and keep warm. Press Sauté and whisk the slurry into the cooking liquid. Bring to a full boil, whisking constantly, and cook until the sauce has thickened to your desired consistency. Serve the thickened sauce over the meat and rice.

For a traditional Caribbean side dish, take 1 (15-ounce, 420 g) can of gluten-free black beans, rinsed and drained, and fold them into a bowl of cooked white rice. Serve hot.

2 Return the meat to the pot, nestling it into the liquids. Add the bay leaves, close and lock the lid, making sure the steam release handle is in the sealing position. Cook on high pressure for 65 minutes. When it is finished, release the pressure naturally for 12 minutes, then turn the steam release handle to venting, releasing any remaining steam. Unlock the lid and open it carefully.

3 Discard the bay leaves. Transfer the meat to a bowl and cut or shred it into bite-size pieces, then return it to the cooking liquid. Stir in the raisins, olives, and vinegar. Taste and adjust the seasoning with salt and pepper if needed. Press Sauté and cook the liquid until slightly reduced, about 10 minutes.

Serve

1 Scoop the rice into serving bowls, top with the beef and some of its juices, and sprinkle the cilantro over the top. Add the beans, if using. Serve immediately.

Mom's Old-Fashioned Pot Roast

DAIRY FREE • SOY FREE • NUT FREE • EGG FREE

There is nothing that smells better when it is cooking than old-fashioned pot roast, packed with tender beef, potatoes, and carrots. With today's pressure cookers, we can have this dinner on the table in much less time than it takes to roast it in the oven, with all the flavor and tenderness we love. If you like, you can serve this over Mashed Potatoes (page 183).

Yield 4 to 6 servings

1 (3-pound, or 1.4 kg) boneless chuck roast

¾ teaspoon kosher or fine sea salt

½ teaspoon freshly ground black pepper

2 tablespoons (30 ml) olive oil

2 cups (470 ml) beef stock (page 212)

½ cup (120 ml) dry red wine or water (see Note, page 133)

1 large onion, coarsely chopped

1 clove garlic, minced

2 bay leaves

1 teaspoon dried rosemary leaves

3 large russet potatoes, peeled and cut into large chunks

4 large carrots, trimmed and cut into large chunks

¼ cup (60 ml) cool water

2 tablespoons (16 g) cornstarch or potato starch

⅓ cup (50 g) frozen peas (optional)

2 tablespoons (6 g) finely chopped fresh parsley

1 Pat the meat dry with paper towels and season with the salt and pepper. Press Sauté and pour the oil into the inner pot. When the oil is shimmering, add the meat and brown on both sides, about 5 minutes per side. Add the stock and wine, stirring to release any browned bits on the bottom of the pan. Stir in the onion, garlic, bay leaves, and rosemary. Press Cancel.

2 Close and lock the lid, making sure the steam release handle is in the sealing position. Cook on high pressure for 70 minutes. When it is finished, allow the pot to naturally release the pressure for 12 minutes, then turn the steam release handle to venting, releasing any remaining steam. Unlock the lid and open it carefully.

3 Quickly add the potatoes and carrots to the pot, replace the lid, set the steam release handle to sealing, bring back to pressure, and cook on high pressure for 3 minutes. Move the handle to venting and release the steam. Unlock the lid and open it carefully.

4 Using a slotted spoon and tongs, transfer the meat and vegetables to a platter. Discard the bay leaves and tent with foil to keep warm. Press Cancel.

5 In a small bowl, whisk together the water and cornstarch. While whisking, slowly pour the cornstarch slurry into the cooking liquid until fully blended. Press Sauté and bring the liquid in the pot to a boil, whisking constantly. Cook until thickened, about 1 minute, then taste and adjust the seasonings if needed. Press Cancel.

6 Stir in the peas, then return the meat and vegetables to the pot, stirring into the sauce. Place the lid on the pot and let sit for 4 minutes, or until peas are thawed and the meat is heated through. Scoop the meat and vegetables into bowls with some of the sauce, sprinkle with the chopped parsley, and serve.

Notes: Some people like tomato in their pot roast cooking liquid. If you want, you can whisk 2 tablespoons (30 g) tomato paste concentrate into the stock before adding the aromatics and seasonings.

Tacos al Pastor with Pineapple Salsa

GLUTEN FREE • DAIRY FREE • SOY FREE • NUT FREE • EGG FREE

Carnitas may get the bulk of the glory when it comes to pork tacos, but my personal favorite style is al pastor. The combination of savory, tender pork with bright, sweet pineapple is captivating. Simple seasonings and a cook time of under an hour make this an easy meal to get on the table any day of the week. Give this a try and you may become a convert, too.

Yield 8 to 10 servings

For the pork filling

2 tablespoons (30 ml) vegetable oil

3 to 4 pounds (1362 to 1816 g) boneless pork shoulder, visible fat trimmed, cut into 2-inch (5 cm) cubes

1 cup (165 g) pineapple chunks, well drained, cut into small pieces

1 small red onion, minced

1½ cups (355 ml) orange juice or water

Juice of 2 limes

3 tablespoons (24 g) chili powder

1 tablespoon (8 g) chipotle powder

1 teaspoon garlic powder (*not* garlic salt)

1 teaspoon ground cumin

1 teaspoon kosher or fine sea salt

1 teaspoon freshly ground black pepper

For the pineapple salsa

1½ cups (248 g) fresh pineapple cubes (if you cannot find fresh pineapple, use canned pineapple packed in water and drain well)

1 red bell pepper, seeded and finely chopped

½ small red onion, finely chopped

1 to 2 jalapeño peppers, seeded and minced

Juice of 1 to 2 limes, to taste

1 tablespoon (15 ml) olive oil

Chopped fresh cilantro, to taste

Sea salt and freshly ground black pepper, to taste

For assembly

Gluten-free corn tortillas, such as Mission brand (see Note)

Chopped fresh cilantro (optional)

Note: Be sure to look for gluten-free corn tortillas. Most corn tortillas in the United States have wheat added to them. Mission brand carries a line of gluten-free tortillas that are very good. If you have any questions about a company's production practices or possible cross-contamination, contact the manufacturer. Also, they may change the ingredients at any time without notice. It always pays to read the labels.

Pork

1 Press Sauté on your pressure cooker and add the oil to the inner pot. When the oil is hot, add a portion of the pork cubes, and brown on all sides. Use a slotted spoon to transfer the meat to a plate and repeat with the remaining pork, working in batches. When it is all browned, place all the meat in the inner pot and add the pineapple, onion, orange and lime juices, chili and chipotle powders, garlic powder, and cumin. Stir to be sure there is nothing stuck to the bottom of the pot.

2 Close and lock the lid, making sure the steam release handle is in the sealing position. Cook on high pressure for 45 minutes. When it is finished, release the pressure naturally for 10 minutes, then quick release the remaining steam by moving the handle to venting. Unlock the lid and open it carefully.

3 Use a slotted spoon to transfer the pork to a large bowl. Use two forks to shred or cut into bite-size cubes. Pour 1 to 2 cups (235 to 470 ml) of the cooking liquid over the pork to keep it moist. Add the salt and pepper, taste, and adjust the seasonings.

Pineapple Salsa

1 In a bowl, combine the pineapple, bell pepper, onion, jalapeños, lime juice, olive oil, and cilantro. Taste and add salt and pepper as desired. Can be made a day or two in advance.

Assembly

1 Fill the corn tortillas with the pork filling and add the pineapple salsa on top. Sprinkle with additional chopped cilantro, if desired, and serve.

Tender BBQ Pulled Pork with Ranch Slaw

GLUTEN FREE • NUT FREE

A classic main course served at barbecues and picnics all summer long, this pulled pork makes the perfect sandwiches for all your guests. The slaw adds a wonderful crunch in every bite and the creaminess of the dressing blends beautifully with the sauce on the pork. This is delightfully messy to eat, so be sure to have plenty of napkins on hand and wet wipes to clean up little hands and faces!

Yield 8 to 10 servings

For the pork

3 tablespoons (45 ml) olive or vegetable oil

2 tablespoons (16 g) smoked paprika

2 tablespoons (25 g) brown sugar

1 tablespoon (8 g) chili powder (Penzeys and McCormick have gluten-free offerings)

2 teaspoons (1 g) dried oregano

1 teaspoon ground cumin

1 teaspoon kosher or fine sea salt

½ teaspoon black pepper

½ teaspoon onion powder

¼ teaspoon garlic powder

4 pounds (1816 g) boneless pork shoulder or butt, cut into large chunks

2 cups (470 ml) chicken stock (page 213)

1 bell pepper, seeded and chopped

1 small onion, chopped

1 to 2 cups (235 to 470 ml) barbecue sauce (Stubb's entire line is gluten free, pick your favorite)

For the dressing

1 cup (235 ml) low-fat buttermilk

½ cup (120 g) low-fat mayonnaise

1 teaspoon freshly squeezed lemon juice

¼ teaspoon very finely minced garlic

2 teaspoons (1 g) minced fresh chives

½ teaspoon dry mustard powder

1½ teaspoons thyme leaves

¼ teaspoon dried dill weed

Kosher or fine sea salt and black pepper, to taste

For the slaw

1 medium head green cabbage, preferably Napa cabbage, thinly sliced

Kosher salt

1 red bell pepper, cored and finely chopped

3 carrots, peeled and shredded

½ small red onion, very finely chopped

For serving

Gluten-free hamburger buns or sliced bread, such as Udi's brand

(continued)

To convert this to Hawaiian Kalua Pork, combine ¾ cup (180 ml) water mixed with 2 teaspoons (10 ml) liquid smoke (Wright's brand is gluten free) and 2 tablespoons (25 g) brown sugar in the bottom of the inner pot. Cut the pork into chunks, place in the pot, and sprinkle with 1 tablespoon (18 g) Alaea Red Hawaiian Sea Salt or 1½ teaspoons kosher salt. Cook on high pressure for 60 minutes with a 15-minute natural release. Shred the pork and add a little of the cooking liquid, tossing to combine. Serve with white rice (page 82) and a mango salsa.

Pork

1 In a bowl, combine the oil, paprika, brown sugar, chili powder, oregano, cumin, salt, pepper, onion powder, and garlic powder to make a paste. Smear over all sides of the pieces of pork. Pour the chicken stock into the inner pot and add the bell pepper and onion. Nestle the pork pieces into the liquid.

2 Close and lock the lid, making sure the steam release handle is in the sealing position. Cook on high pressure for 60 minutes. When it is finished, release the pressure naturally for 14 minutes, then turn the steam release handle to venting, releasing any remaining steam. When the float pin drops, unlock the lid and open it carefully.

3 Use a slotted spoon to transfer the pork, onions, and bell pepper to a baking sheet with sides. Reserve the cooking liquid. Use two forks to shred the meat, discarding large pieces of fat.

4 Pour the barbecue sauce into a bowl and add a little of the cooking liquid to thin slightly. Pour this mixture over the shredded pork, tossing to coat all the pieces. Transfer to a saucepan and keep warm over low heat, covered, stirring regularly. Add a little more of the cooking juices if the mixture starts to dry out.

5 This is also great made ahead. Refrigerate, covered, for a few days or freeze for longer storage.

Dressing

1 In a medium bowl, combine the buttermilk, mayonnaise, and lemon juice. Whisk in the garlic, chives, mustard, thyme, and dill. Cover and refrigerate for at least 2 hours to give the flavors time to blend. Taste and adjust the seasonings with salt and pepper as desired.

Slaw

1 Place the sliced cabbage in a colander and liberally sprinkle with kosher salt. Toss gently to distribute the salt. Place the colander over a large bowl and set aside for 30 to 45 minutes. The salt will leach out most of the water, leaving the cabbage crispier. Rinse the cabbage well under cool running water, making sure the salt has been removed. Set the colander aside again to drain thoroughly, shaking it occasionally.

2 Transfer the drained cabbage to a very large mixing bowl and add the bell pepper, carrots, and onion. Toss to evenly distribute the ingredients and add ½ to ¾ cup (120 to 180 ml) of the dressing, tossing to evenly coat everything. Taste and adjust the seasonings as desired. Cover and refrigerate for at least 30 minutes. If any extra liquid accumulates while it is resting, drain before serving.

Serve

1 Lightly toast the gluten-free hamburger buns if you like. Pile on some of the pulled pork and top with the slaw. Serve immediately.

Notes: If you are looking for a shortcut, you can buy prepared slaw or a bag of sliced cabbage and add in your own grated carrots, bell pepper, and red onion or whatever vegetables you like. Then dress it with the Ranch dressing or whichever slaw dressing your family prefers.

Have trouble finding gluten-free buns in your area? You can also serve this wrapped in lettuce leaves. The crunch of the lettuce is a perfect compliment to the tender pulled pork.

BBQ Baby Back Ribs

GLUTEN FREE • DAIRY FREE • SOY FREE • NUT FREE • EGG FREE

Tender barbecued ribs are a skill that professional grill masters spend years perfecting. Trying to control live fire can be challenging. But if you put those same ribs in an electric pressure cooker, you get perfectly cooked ribs every time with no worry that the weather will interfere and no need to stand watch for hours at the grill. Using a good barbecue sauce, sprinkling with smoked paprika, and broiling at the end help get the flavors close to what you get on the grill with fall-off-the-bone tenderness.

Yield 2 to 3 servings

1 (3-pound, or 1.4 kg) rack of baby back ribs

2 tablespoons (30 g) brown sugar

1 tablespoon (6 g) smoked paprika

1 tablespoon (6 g) chili powder (Penzeys and McCormick brands clearly mark their products for allergens)

1 tablespoon (18 g) kosher or fine sea salt

2 teaspoons (1 g) dried thyme leaves

2 teaspoons (2 g) onion powder (*not* onion salt)

1 teaspoon garlic powder (*not* garlic salt)

1 teaspoon freshly ground black pepper

Your favorite gluten-free barbecue sauce (Stubb's brand is gluten free)

For the cooking pot
1¼ cups (295 ml) water

1 Lay the ribs bone side up on a baking sheet and remove the membrane covering the surface. Place the trivet in the bottom of the inner pot and pour in the water.

2 In a small bowl, mix together the brown sugar, smoked paprika, chili powder, salt, thyme, onion powder, garlic powder, and pepper. Rub the seasoning mix over all sides of the ribs. Stand the ribs around the edges of the inner pot.

3 Close and lock the lid, making sure the steam release handle is in the sealing position. Cook on high pressure for 17 minutes. When it is finished, release the pressure naturally for 10 minutes, then move the handle to venting and release the remaining steam. Unlock the lid and open it carefully. Press Cancel.

4 Use tongs to transfer the ribs to a clean baking sheet. Preheat the broiler. Lightly brush one side of the ribs with barbecue sauce. Slide the ribs under the broiler for a few minutes until the sauce is bubbling. Flip the pieces over and repeat the broiling, brushing with more sauce. Watch carefully so the ribs don't burn.

5 Serve while hot, passing additional sauce at the table.

ASIAN FAVORITES

Save yourself from hunger on busy nights without picking up the phone and ordering takeout. Your pressure cooker can help you prepare completely gluten-free, delicious Asian-inspired dishes at home.

For many people with gluten sensitivities, in addition to avoiding the usual grains like wheat, barley, and pastas, they also have to navigate the hidden gluten in many processed foods. The biggest culprits in Asian foods are soy sauce, seitan (which is pure gluten), and many of our favorite Asian sauces. We knew we wanted to address this issue (partly because we love Asian dishes), so we substituted coconut aminos for soy sauce in the majority of these recipes. The flavor isn't quite the same, but it does give you the deep umami taste you normally get from soy sauce. Coconut aminos are made from the coconut blossom nectar of coconut palms. The nectar is fermented and blended with sea salt. Not only are coconut aminos healthier for you (73 percent less sodium than soy sauce), but they are also gluten free, soy

free, kosher, and vegan. There are some brands that carry gluten-free Asian-style sauces, and you'll see a few in this chapter. For the most part, we've made our own sauces for these dishes, so you can rest easy knowing they're all gluten free!

With flavors from Sichuan, Hong Kong, Thailand, the Philippines, and a few Chinese American favorites, this chapter contains many popular restaurant classics, so you can enjoy a wide variety of different cuisines without leaving home.

Recipes

Kung Pao Chicken

GLUTEN FREE • SOY-FREE OPTION •
DAIRY FREE • EGG FREE

One of the most popular Chinese dishes in America is kung pao chicken. The sauce is salty, sweet, sour, and spicy all at once. It's hard to resist. A simple marinade gives the chicken an additional depth of flavor. Serve this dish over rice and toss a few toasted sesame seeds on top! If you're not a fan of zucchini, feel free to swap it out for carrots or asparagus— any seasonal vegetable will do. Leave out the red chile peppers if you aren't a spice fan, or if you like it spicy, add a few more. Customizing this dish to your own liking is fun and easy!

Yield 6 servings

For the marinade

2 teaspoons (6 g) cornstarch

1 tablespoon (15 ml) coconut aminos (or gluten-free soy sauce)

2 teaspoons (10 ml) rice wine vinegar

1½ pounds (680 g) boneless, skinless chicken breasts, cut into 1-inch (2.5 cm) pieces

3 tablespoons (45 ml) vegetable oil

For the sauce

1 tablespoon (15 ml) red wine vinegar

1 teaspoon sesame oil

½ cup (120 ml) coconut aminos (or gluten-free soy sauce)

¼ cup (60 ml) water

3 tablespoons (60 g) honey

⅓ cup (80 g) gluten-free hoisin sauce (San-J brand is gluten free)

4 cloves garlic, minced

2 teaspoons (6 g) grated fresh ginger

½ teaspoon ground Sichuan pepper

Vegetables

1 leek, peeled, cleaned well, and thinly sliced

1 zucchini, cut in half horizontally and sliced into ½-inch (1.3 cm) pieces

1 red bell pepper, seeded and cut into bite-size pieces

1 green bell pepper, seeded and cut into bite-size pieces

2 teaspoons (4 g) red pepper flakes (or to taste)

For the cornstarch slurry

2 tablespoons (16 g) cornstarch

3 tablespoons (45 ml) water

For serving and garnish

½ cup (60 g) roasted, unsalted cashews

White rice (page 82), for serving

3 scallions, trimmed and sliced on the bias, white and green parts, for garnish

Toasted sesame seeds, for garnish

Marinade

1 In a medium bowl, whisk together the cornstarch, coconut aminos, and rice wine vinegar until the cornstarch is dissolved. Add the chicken pieces and stir to coat. Let stand for 10 minutes at room temperature.

2 Press Sauté on your electric pressure cooker. When the inner pot is hot, add the oil. Cook the chicken in batches (placing the browned chicken on a paper towel-lined plate) for 3 to 4 minutes on each side, until golden brown. Once all the chicken is browned, add the pieces back to the pot. Discard the remaining marinade and quickly wash out the marinade bowl so you can use it again.

Sauce

1 Combine the vinegar, sesame oil, coconut aminos, water, honey, hoisin sauce, garlic, ginger, and Sichuan pepper in the bowl and stir to combine. Pour the sauce over the chicken in the pot.

2 Close and lock the lid, making sure the steam release handle is in the sealing position. Cook on high pressure for 6 minutes. When the cook time is finished, allow a 20-minute natural release, then do a quick release to vent any remaining steam. When the float pin drops, unlock the lid and open it carefully. Transfer the chicken to a large serving bowl.

Vegetables

1 Press Sauté and add the leek, zucchini, bell peppers, and red pepper flakes. Allow to cook for 5 minutes, until tender.

Cornstarch Slurry

1 Combine the cornstarch and water to make a slurry. Add the slurry to the pot and allow the sauce to thicken, about 2 minutes.

Serving and Garnish

1 Return the chicken to the pot and add the cashews. Cook for an additional 2 minutes, or until everything is warmed through.

2 Serve over rice and top with the scallions and toasted sesame seeds.

The Best Beef and Broccoli

GLUTEN FREE • SOY-FREE OPTION • NUT FREE • DAIRY FREE • EGG FREE

This flavorful recipe is perfect when you are craving Chinese food but don't want to go out. Coconut aminos take the place of soy sauce in this recipe. It's a great gluten-free option with much less sodium than regular soy sauce. You should be able to find coconut aminos in the international aisle of most grocery stores. If you can't, it's widely available online. Serve this beef and broccoli with jasmine rice or spiralized vegetables.

Yield 4 servings

2 teaspoons (10 ml) olive oil

2 pounds (908 g) boneless beef chuck roast, trimmed and cut into thin strips

1 medium onion, finely chopped

6 cloves garlic, minced

1¾ cups (410 ml) beef stock (page 212)

¼ cup (60 ml) coconut aminos (or gluten-free soy sauce)

¼ cup (60 ml) gluten-free oyster sauce (Lee Kum Kee Panda Brand is gluten free)

¼ cup (55 g) brown sugar

1 tablespoon (15 ml) sesame oil

½ teaspoon red pepper flakes

¼ cup (60 ml) water

3 tablespoons (24 g) cornstarch

1 pound (454 g) broccoli florets

1 Press Sauté on your electric pressure cooker. When the inner pot is hot, add the olive oil. When the oil is hot, add the meat and brown in batches until all the strips have been cooked. Transfer the meat to a plate.

2 Add the chopped onion to the pot with the remaining meat juices and oil. Sauté for 2 minutes, or until the onion starts to soften. Add the garlic and cook for an additional 30 seconds, until fragrant.

3 Add the beef stock, coconut aminos, oyster sauce, brown sugar, sesame oil, and red pepper flakes to the pot. Whisk until the sauce is bubbly and the brown sugar is dissolved. Press Cancel.

4 Add the browned beef back to the pot. Close and lock the lid, making sure the steam release handle is in the sealing position. Cook on high pressure for 12 minutes. When the cook time is finished, use the quick release method by opening the release knob and venting all the steam. When the float pin drops, unlock the lid and open it carefully. Press Cancel.

5 In a small bowl, combine the cornstarch and water; stir until smooth. Press Sauté and add the cornstarch mixture to the pot. Stir until the sauce comes to a boil and thickens. Press Cancel.

6 Add the broccoli and close the lid. Allow the broccoli to warm in the residual heat for 3 to 5 minutes.

7 Remove the lid, stir, and serve.

Chicken
Lo Mein

GLUTEN FREE • SOY-FREE OPTION •
DAIRY FREE • EGG FREE

Have your favorite takeout dinner at home for a fraction of the cost! This one-pot dinner is packed with vegetables, chicken, and thick, chewy noodles all cooked in a gluten-free sauce. While this dish is usually done in a wok, there is something wonderful about being able to put everything in a pot, press a button, and walk away.

Yield 6 servings

To make this dish vegetarian, omit the chicken and reduce the cooking time to 3 minutes.

1½ pounds (680 g) chicken breast, cut into bite-size pieces

2 teaspoons (12 g) salt

1 teaspoon black pepper

1 tablespoon (15 ml) sesame oil

1 medium onion, sliced

1 tablespoon (10 g) minced garlic

1 pound (454 g) gluten-free linguini or thick rice noodles

1½ cups (355 ml) chicken stock (page 213)

¼ cup (60 ml) coconut aminos (or gluten-free soy sauce)

⅓ cup (80 ml) gluten-free hoisin sauce (San-J has a gluten-free version)

2 tablespoons (30 ml) gluten-free oyster sauce (San-J has a gluten-free version)

2 teaspoons (10 ml) freshly squeezed lemon juice

1 large red bell pepper, seeded and cut into thin strips

2 large carrots, peeled and cut into matchsticks

1 cup (75 g) snow peas

2 cups (150 g) sliced mushrooms

1 cup (50 g) bean sprouts

¼ cup (25 g) sliced scallions, green parts only, for garnish

1 Press Sauté on your electric pressure cooker. While the pot is heating, season the chicken with salt and pepper. When the inner pot is hot, add the sesame oil.

2 Add the chicken to the pot and sauté for 6 minutes, or until golden brown on all sides. Add the onions and cook until they just begin to turn translucent, 3 minutes. Add the garlic and cook for 30 seconds, until fragrant. Press Cancel.

3 Break the linguini noodles in half and layer in the pot on top of the chicken and onions.

4 In a medium bowl, combine the chicken stock, coconut aminos, hoisin sauce, oyster sauce, and lemon juice. Pour the sauce over the chicken but don't stir. Layer the bell pepper and carrots on top of the chicken.

5 Close and lock the lid, making sure the steam release handle is in the sealing position. Cook on high pressure for 6 minutes. When the cook time is finished, press Cancel and use the quick release method by turning the release handle to the open position and venting all the steam. When the float pin drops, unlock the lid and open it carefully.

6 Add the snow peas, mushrooms, and bean sprouts to the pot. Stir until covered in sauce. Replace the lid and let sit for 5 minutes in the residual heat to warm the vegetables.

7 Serve in big bowls, garnished with scallions.

Sweet-and-Sour Pork

GLUTEN FREE • SOY-FREE OPTION •
NUT FREE • DAIRY FREE • EGG FREE

This easy, bright-flavored dish combines tender pork, sweet pineapple, and crisp vegetables with a home-made sweet-and-sour sauce. Instead of using the tradi-tional deep-fry coating that requires flour, brown the pork pieces until they are extra crispy. You'll still get the crunch, but without the accompanying gluten. The dazzling red color of the sauce gets its shine and a bit of its sweetness from ketch-up. Some ketchups contain trace amounts of gluten because the vinegar they use is distilled from wheat products, so be sure to look for ketchup that is certified gluten free.

Yield 4 servings

If you have trouble finding coconut aminos, you can sub-stitute your favorite gluten-free soy sauce. Kikkoman and Lee Kum Kim Panda Brand are both good options.

1 tablespoon (15 ml) vegetable oil

1½ pounds (680 g) pork steak, cut into 1-inch (2.5 cm) pieces

½ cup (120 g) gluten-free ketchup (Not Ketchup Fruitchup brand is gluten free)

⅓ cup (80 ml) apple cider vinegar (Bragg brand is gluten free)

⅓ cup (80 ml) pineapple juice (reserved from can of pineapple chunks)

2 tablespoons (25 g) brown sugar

1 tablespoon (15 ml) coconut aminos (or gluten-free soy sauce)

2 teaspoons (6 g) freshly minced ginger

1 cup (235 ml) water, divided

1 large onion, cut into chunks

1 medium red bell pepper, cored and cut into chunks

1 medium green bell pepper, cored and cut into chunks

1 cup (175 g) pineapple chunks

3 tablespoons (24 g) cornstarch

Cooked rice (page 82), for serving

1 Press Sauté on your electric pressure cooker. When the inner pot is hot, add the oil and cook the pork pieces until browned and crispy on each side. You may need to work batches.

2 In a medium bowl, whisk the ketchup, vinegar, pineapple juice, brown sugar, coconut aminos, ginger, and ¾ cup (180 ml) of the water until smooth. Return the browned pieces of pork to the pot and cover with the sauce.

3 Close and lock the lid, making sure the steam release handle is in the sealing position. Cook on high pressure for 5 minutes. When it is finished, allow an 8-minute natural release, then do a quick release to vent any remaining steam. When the float pin drops, unlock the lid and open it carefully.

4 Remove the pork from the pot with a slotted spoon. Place in a serving bowl and cover with foil. Press Cancel.

5 With all the liquid still in the pot, press Sauté and add the onion, bell peppers, and pineap-ple chunks to the bottom of the pan. Gently simmer for about 5 minutes, or until the vegeta-bles are just beginning to soften.

6 In a small bowl, combine the cornstarch and remaining ¼ cup (60 ml) water and whisk until smooth. Slowly pour the dissolved cornstarch into the pot and stir to combine.

7 Continue cooking the sauce, stirring constantly, until it has thickened to the desired consistency, 2 to 3 minutes. Return the crispy pork pieces to the pot to warm through and coat in the sauce. Serve over hot rice.

Vegetable Pad Thai

GLUTEN FREE • DAIRY FREE

Pad Thai is arguably one of the most popular Asian dishes in America. This is a vegetable pad Thai, but you can add precooked chicken, beef, or pork. It's important to do a quick release as soon as the cook time is finished or the noodles will over-cook and turn to mush. This flavorful and simple one-pot dinner goes together in no time, making it perfect for a quick weeknight meal.

Yield 4 servings

You can find sweetened radish and dried shrimp in most Asian markets. If you can't find it, just omit it. It will still taste great.

½ cup (120 ml) fish sauce

2 tablespoons (30 ml) fresh lime juice

2 tablespoons (30 ml) rice wine vinegar

3 tablespoons (45 ml) coconut aminos

⅓ cup (65 g) sugar

1 tablespoon (15 ml) vegetable oil

1 medium onion, thinly sliced

4 large cloves garlic, minced

10 ounces (280 g) pad Thai rice noodles

12 ounces (340 g) extra-firm tofu, sliced

2 cups (470 ml) vegetable stock (page 214)

2 tablespoons (14 g) shredded sweetened radish

1 teaspoon dried shrimp

1 cup (50 g) bean sprouts

1 medium carrot, peeled and shaved into ribbons

2 large eggs

¼ cup (38 g) chopped unsalted roasted peanuts

3 scallions, trimmed and cut into 3-inch (7.5 cm) julienne strips

1 medium lime, cut into 8 wedges

1 In a medium bowl, whisk together the fish sauce, lime juice, vinegar, coconut aminos, and sugar until the sugar is completely dissolved. Set aside.

2 Press Sauté on your electric pressure cooker. When the inner pot is hot, add the oil. Sauté the onion until just translucent, 2 to 3 minutes. Add the garlic and cook an additional 30 seconds, until fragrant.

3 Pour the fish sauce mixture over the onions and garlic. Add the rice noodles and tofu to the pot. Add the stock, radishes, and shrimp, but do not stir. Submerge the noodles as much as possible.

4 Close and lock the lid, making sure the steam release handle is in the sealing position. Cook on high pressure for 3 minutes. When the cook time is finished, use the quick release method by opening the release handle and venting all the steam. When the float pin drops, unlock the lid and open it carefully.

5 Add the bean sprouts and carrots to the pot. Replace the lid and let the vegetables warm through, 5 minutes.

6 While the vegetables are warming, whisk the eggs in a small bowl and scramble in a small frying pan. Stir the warm eggs into the pad Thai.

7 Serve in big bowls garnished with the peanuts, scallions, and lime wedges.

Chicken Adobo

GLUTEN FREE • SOY-FREE OPTION • NUT FREE • DAIRY FREE • EGG FREE

This recipe is a Filipino favorite; in fact, it's the national dish of the Philippines. There is much debate in the Philippines over which protein is better: chicken, pork or fish. We've opted for chicken in our version. The vinegar in the marinade is the star of the dish and lends to its signature flavor. Don't leave out the whole peppercorns or the crazy amount of garlic. They are requirements! Another great thing about this dish is that the rice cooks inside the pot with the chicken and sauce, making it a complete, all-in-one meal.

Yield 4 servings

For the marinade

¾ cup (180 ml) coconut aminos (or gluten-free soy sauce)

⅓ cup (80 ml) apple cider vinegar

2 tablespoons (30 ml) fish sauce

1 tablespoon (12 g) brown sugar

2 tablespoons (16 g) freshly grated ginger

2 teaspoons (3 g) whole black peppercorns

1½ teaspoons crushed red pepper flakes

For the chicken

2 ½ pounds (1135 g) boneless, skinless chicken thighs

2 tablespoons (30 ml) vegetable oil

1 large onion, roughly chopped

16 whole cloves garlic, peeled

6 bay leaves

For the rice

1½ cups (355 ml) water

1½ cups (270 g) jasmine rice

⅓ cup (35 g) sliced scallions, for garnish

Marinade

1 In a medium bowl, combine the marinade ingredients and whisk together.

Chicken

1 Add the chicken pieces to the bowl, turning each piece to evenly coat the chicken with the sauce. Leave the chicken in the bowl and set aside. Let the chicken marinate for 30 minutes.

2 When the chicken is almost done marinating, press Sauté on your electric pressure cooker. When the inner pot is hot, add the oil. Add the onion and cook until just beginning to soften, 4 minutes. Add the garlic and cook an additional 30 seconds, until fragrant.

3 Add the chicken and marinade to the pot with the onions and garlic. Add the bay leaves.

4 Nestle a long-legged trivet over the chicken pieces, making sure the legs of the trivet are touching the bottom of the pot. Press Cancel.

Rice

1 Place the rice in a fine-mesh strainer and rinse under cold water until the water runs clear, about 1 minute. Let the rice drain completely and begin to dry out a little. Add the drained rice to a 1½-quart (1.4 L) round casserole dish or 7-inch (18 cm) cake pan. Cover the rice with the 1½ cups (355 ml) fresh water. Cover the top of the dish with aluminum foil, crimping the edges to seal.

2 Using a foil sling (see page 18), gently lower the pan of rice on top of the trivet in the pot. It should just fit nicely inside and not touch the lid when the pot is closed.

3 Close and lock the lid, making sure the steam release handle is in the sealing position. Cook on high pressure for 15 minutes. When it is finished, allow a natural release for 10 minutes, then turn the release handle to vent any remaining steam. When the float pin drops, unlock the lid and open it carefully.

4 Use oven mitts to remove the bowl of rice. Set aside. Remove the trivet from the pot with tongs. Press Cancel.

5 Transfer the chicken pieces to a foil-lined baking sheet. Strain the sauce through a fine-mesh colander to get rid of the bay leaves, peppercorns, and any unwanted bits that might have fallen from the chicken. Try to pull out as many of the garlic pieces as possible and add them to the plate with the chicken. Return the sauce to the inner pot of your pressure cooker.

6 Press Sauté and allow the sauce to simmer and reduce for 10 to 15 minutes, or until it reaches your desired consistency. Stir often to ensure the sauce doesn't burn.

7 While the sauce is simmering, place the chicken under the broiler for 6 to 10 minutes to crisp up the skin. Keep an eye on it so it doesn't get too crispy!

8 When the chicken is finished and the sauce has reduced enough to your liking, divide the rice among 4 bowls, place the chicken on top of the rice, and drizzle the sauce over the top. Serve with the sliced scallions.

If you wish to use the more traditional bone-in chicken legs and thighs for this recipe, increase the cooking time by 3 minutes.

Asian-Style BBQ Pork Ribs

GLUTEN FREE • SOY FREE • NUT FREE • DAIRY FREE • EGG FREE

This is an old family recipe adapted for the pressure cooker. This is the dish that brings the adult children back to visit for dinner. It has a garlicky, spicy marinade that goes beautifully with pork, but also works well with chicken. If you are short on time, skip the marinade process and simply put everything in the pressure cooker. If you do, add an extra 2 minutes to the cook time. It will still be wonderful, but the flavor won't be quite as deep as if it were marinated overnight.

Yield 4 servings

For the marinade

3 tablespoons (36 g) sugar

⅓ cup plus 1 tablespoon (95 ml) coconut aminos

3 tablespoons (45 ml) red wine vinegar

1 teaspoon salt

1½ teaspoons black pepper

1½ teaspoons ground ginger

½ teaspoon cayenne pepper

2 tablespoons (20 g) minced garlic

1 tablespoon (11 g) stone-ground mustard

1½ teaspoons red pepper flakes

¼ cup (60 ml) water

For the ribs

3 pounds (1362 g) boneless, country-style pork ribs

Marinade

1 In a large bowl, combine all the marinade ingredients.

Ribs

1 Add the ribs, cover, and marinate in the refrigerator for 12 to 24 hours.

2 When you are ready to cook, remove the ribs from the refrigerator and put everything (ribs and all the marinade) into the inner pot of your electric pressure cooker.

3 Close and lock the lid, making sure the steam release handle is in the sealing position. Cook on high pressure for 40 minutes. When the cook time is finished, allow a 15-minute natural release, then do a quick release to vent any remaining steam. When the float pin drops, unlock the lid and open it carefully.

4 With a slotted spoon, remove the ribs to a serving plate. Serve over hot rice. Use the flavorful cooking liquid as a sauce to pour over the ribs.

Taking the ribs straight from the refrigerator to the pressure cooker means it will take longer to come to pressure. The colder temperature difference takes longer to heat. Be sure to allow extra time for this when you are planning dinner.

Honey Garlic Chicken

GLUTEN FREE • DAIRY FREE • SOY-FREE OPTION • NUT FREE • EGG FREE

Savory, sweet, tender, and juicy chicken legs are smothered in the most amazing honey garlic sauce. You may find yourself making this sauce to use with other things, too. It's just that good. Simple ingredients means it's important to use the best-quality ingredients you can find. Try an orange blossom honey or any other local artisan honey for a unique spin on this dish!

Yield 4 servings

1 tablespoon (2 g) dried thyme

1 tablespoon (2 g) dried oregano

¼ teaspoon cayenne pepper

⅓ cup (107 g) honey

6 cloves garlic, minced

½ cup (120 ml) coconut aminos (or gluten-free soy sauce)

¼ cup (60 ml) chicken stock (page 213)

Salt and freshly ground pepper, to taste

1 tablespoon (15 ml) sesame seed oil

8 bone-in, skinless chicken legs

2 tablespoons (16 g) cornstarch

2 tablespoons (30 ml) cold water

½ tablespoon toasted sesame seeds, for garnish

Sliced scallion, for garnish

1 In a small mixing bowl, combine the thyme, oregano, cayenne pepper, honey, garlic, coconut aminos, stock, and salt and pepper; mix until well combined and set aside.

2 Press Sauté on your electric pressure cooker. When the inner pot is hot, add the sesame oil to the pot. Season the chicken with salt and pepper; sauté until golden brown, 3 to 4 minutes per side.

3 Add the prepared honey garlic sauce to the pot, covering the chicken completely. Close and lock the lid, making sure the steam release handle is in the sealing position. Cook on high pressure for 18 minutes.

4 When the cook time is finished, press Cancel. Allow a 10-minute natural release, then do a quick release to vent any remaining steam. When the float pin drops, unlock the lid and open it carefully. Transfer the chicken to a serving plate.

5 Stir the sauce. Press Sauté. In a small bowl, combine the cornstarch and cold water. Add the cornstarch slurry to the sauce in the pot and stir continuously for 2 minutes, or until the sauce thickens.

6 To serve, spoon the sauce over the chicken. Garnish with the toasted sesame seeds and scallions.

Japanese Beef Curry

GLUTEN FREE • SOY-FREE OPTION •
EGG FREE • DAIRY FREE • NUT FREE

Kare-raisu, or Japanese curry rice, is a thick, curried stew of potatoes, carrots, and onions, served over rice. Slightly sweet and often spicy, it is a very common dish in Japan. Every household has its own variation, adding different vegetables, swapping the beef for other meats, or creating different levels of spice to meet their family's preferences. The electric pressure cooker makes quick work of this dish, which normally takes a few hours to simmer and thicken. To be traditional, kare-raisu should be topped with pickled shallots and eaten with a spoon.

Yield 4 servings

1 tablespoon (15 ml) vegetable oil

1 pound (454 g) boneless beef chuck shoulder roast, cut into 1-inch (2.5 cm) cubes

½ onion, chopped

2 carrots, peeled and chopped

1 turnip, peeled and cubed

4 cloves garlic, chopped

1 teaspoon grated ginger

1 large russet potato, cubed

3 cups (705 ml) beef stock (page 212)

1 tablespoon (12 g) brown sugar

1 tablespoon (8 g) curry powder

2 tablespoons (30 g) tomato paste

3 tablespoons (45 ml) coconut aminos (or gluten-free soy sauce)

1 tablespoon (8 g) garam masala

1½ teaspoons salt

½ teaspoon cracked black pepper

¼ teaspoon red pepper flakes

1 cup (190 g) long-grain brown rice

1¼ cups (295 ml) plus 3 table-spoons (45 ml) water, divided

1 tablespoon (8 g) cornstarch

2 teaspoons (1 g) chopped chives

1 lime, cut into 8 wedges

1 Press Sauté on your electric pressure cooker. When the inner pot is hot, add the oil. Brown the cubed beef on all sides, stirring often so the meat doesn't burn. Add the onion, carrots, turnip, garlic, ginger, and potato to the pot. Press Cancel.

2 In a medium bowl, combine the beef stock, brown sugar, curry, tomato paste, coconut aminos, garam masala, salt, pepper, and red pepper flakes. Whisk to combine, then pour over the meat and vegetables in the pressure cooker.

Chicken Congee

GLUTEN FREE • EGG FREE • DAIRY FREE • SOY-FREE OPTION

Also known as jook, congee is often eaten as breakfast. Silky, creamy, and easy on your stomach, congee is perfect any time, day or night. The chicken flavor in this dish is deep and rich thanks to the meat being done in the pressure cooker. This flavorful porridge-like soup is great to make when you have a little bit of rice left in the pantry and don't know what to do with it.

Yield 7 servings

A word of warning: This makes a big batch! It is great to freeze in individual portions.

1 cup (190 g) short-grain gluten-free white rice (such as sushi rice or Arborio rice from Lundberg Family Farms)

1 tablespoon (15 ml) olive oil

1 medium onion, diced

3 stalks celery, including leafy tops, thinly sliced

1 cup (120 g) peeled and diced carrots

6 boneless, skinless chicken thighs, each cut into 4 pieces

1½ tablespoons (12 g) grated fresh ginger

8 cups (1880 ml) chicken stock (page 213)

2 teaspoons (10 ml) coconut aminos (or gluten-free soy sauce)

Scallions, thinly sliced, green parts only, for garnish

1 Place the rice in a fine-mesh strainer and rinse under cold water until the water runs clear, about 1 minute.

2 Press Sauté on your electric pressure cooker. When the inner pot is hot, add the oil. Add the onion, celery, and carrots. Sauté for 3 minutes, or until the vegetables just begin to soften. Press Cancel.

3 Add the chicken, grated ginger, rinsed rice, chicken stock, and coconut aminos to the pot. Make sure the liquid does not go above the maximum fill line.

4 Close and lock the lid, making sure the steam release handle is in the sealing position. Cook on high pressure for 20 minutes. When the cook time is finished, press Cancel and allow a full natural release. Once the float pin drops, you can safely unlock the lid. Open it carefully, being sure to tip the lid away from you to avoid any excess steam.

5 Remove the chicken from the pot. Using two forks, shred the meat and then return to the pot. Stir well to combine.

6 Press Sauté. Stir the congee until it reaches the desired consistency. Taste and adjust the seasonings, adding more coconut aminos or salt, as needed.

7 Serve in big bowls, garnished with plenty of scallions.

Thai Basil Coconut Curry Chicken

GLUTEN FREE • DAIRY FREE • EGG FREE • NUT FREE • SOY FREE

This Thai curry chicken is great for a busy weeknight. The addition of jicama at the end gives the dish a nice, crispy crunch. The jicama also tones down the heat a little bit. Of course, you have the option of kicking up the spice (add more jalapeño) if you like your curry a bit on the spicy side.

Yield 4 servings

- 1 cup (190 g) jasmine rice
- 2 tablespoons (30 ml) olive oil
- 4 boneless, skinless chicken thighs, cut into bite-size pieces
- 1 yellow onion, cut in half and thinly sliced
- 1 jalapeño pepper, seeded and thinly sliced (add more if you like more spice)
- 1 tablespoon (10 g) chopped garlic
- 1 (13.5-ounce, or 378) can full-fat coconut milk
- 1 cup (235 ml) chicken stock (page 213)
- 2 tablespoons (16 g) grated fresh ginger
- 1 teaspoon salt
- 2 tablespoons (16 g) yellow curry powder
- 1½ teaspoons chili powder
- 1 cup (235 ml) plus 1 tablespoon (15 ml) water, divided
- Juice and zest from 1 medium lime
- ½ cup (20 g) chopped fresh Thai basil leaves, divided
- 1 tablespoon (8 g) cornstarch
- ½ cup (65 g) peeled and finely matchstick-cut jicama

1 Place the rice in a fine-mesh strainer and rinse under cold water until the water runs clear, about 1 minute. Set aside to drain.

2 Press Sauté on your electric pressure cooker. When the inner pot is hot, add the oil. Add the chicken pieces and lightly brown on all sides. Add the onion and jalapeño and sauté until just beginning to soften, 2 minutes. Add the garlic and cook an additional 30 seconds, until fragrant. Press Cancel.

3 In a large mixing bowl, whisk together the coconut milk, chicken stock, ginger, salt, curry powder, and chili powder. Pour over the chicken and vegetables in the pressure cooker. Nestle a long-legged trivet over the chicken and curry mixture, making sure all the legs of the trivet are touching the bottom of the pot.

4 In a 7 x 3-inch (18 x 7.6 cm) cake pan, combine the drained rice with 1 cup (235 ml) of the water. Make sure rice is fully submerged in the water. Cover the pan with aluminum foil, crimping the edges gently to seal. Using a foil sling (see page 18), lower the rice pan onto the trivet.

5 Close and lock the lid, making sure the steam release handle is in the sealing position. Cook on high pressure for 15 minutes. When the cook time is finished, do a quick pressure release by carefully moving the sealing handle to venting and allowing all the steam to escape. When the float pin drops, press Cancel, unlock the lid, and open it carefully.

6 Remove the rice pan from the pot using the sling. Set aside. Using tongs, carefully remove the trivet from the pot. Stir the chicken curry mixture. Add the lime juice and zest, along with ⅓ cup (15 g) of the basil leaves.

7 In a small bowl, combine the cornstarch and remaining 1 tablespoon (15 ml) water to form a slurry. Press Sauté and add the cornstarch mixture to the chicken curry. Allow to simmer for 3 to 4 minutes, or until the curry has thickened, stirring often.

8 Stir in the jicama pieces and continue to stir for 1 minute longer. Press Cancel.

9 Divide the cooked rice equally among 4 serving bowls. Top with the curry chicken mixture. Serve with the remaining basil leaves on top.

8 SENSATIONAL SIDE DISHES

The perfect accompaniment to your favorite main dishes, these sensational sides will have you singing with joy over how simple they are to make. There is no need to take up precious space in the oven when you can utilize your pressure cooker to do the work for you. These sides include gluten-free versions of many family favorites, so you can balance dinner with something wholesome and comforting.

Did you know most corn bread recipes have wheat flour in them? It is another sneaky place you will find gluten. We've given you two versions, one sweet (page 180) and one savory (page 188), to enjoy as well as a corn bread stuffing recipe (page 189) that is perfect for holiday entertaining. And don't miss our recipe for a beautiful Roast Turkey Breast with Easy Gravy (page 126)!

Winter holidays aren't the only time to celebrate! We have sensational sides for springtime celebrations, summer festivities, picnics (our Quick and Easy Potato Salad, page 177, is one you will make over and over again!), and fall favorites! Perfect for year-long, gluten-free entertaining!

Recipes

Steamed Broccoli with Cheese Sauce

GLUTEN FREE • SOY FREE • NUT FREE • EGG FREE

We think this spicy broccoli pairs perfectly with a sharp cheddar cheese sauce. It's not a typo to steam your broccoli for 0 minutes. The time it takes your pressure cooker to simply come to pressure is the perfect amount of time to steam all kinds of vegetables. Any kind of cheese sauce normally means creating a roux using flour. For this recipe we've swapped traditional flour for rice flour. Not only does it create a gorgeous roux, but the rice flour is finer than regular flour, giving your cheese sauce a smoother, creamier texture. The recipe is easy to double and you may find yourself making the cheese sauce by itself for any number of other dishes.

Yield 1½ cups (355 ml) cheese sauce, about 6 servings

For the broccoli
2½ cups (175 g) broccoli florets
1 tablespoon (15 ml) olive oil
2 teaspoons (6 g) minced garlic
1 teaspoon red pepper flakes
½ teaspoon salt
½ teaspoon black pepper

For the cheese sauce
3 tablespoons (42 g) unsalted butter
3 tablespoons (24 g) rice flour
1¼ cups (295 ml) milk
2 teaspoons (4 g) garlic powder
1 teaspoon onion powder
1 cup (120 g) shredded sharp cheddar cheese
Salt, to taste (optional)

Broccoli

1 In a large bowl, toss the broccoli florets with the olive oil, minced garlic, red pepper flakes, salt, and pepper. Place a steamer basket in the inner pot of your electric pressure cooker. Pour 1 cup (235 ml) water into the pot. Place the seasoned broccoli in the steamer basket.

2 Close and lock the lid, making sure the steam release handle is in the sealing position. Press Manual and cook on high pressure for 0 (zero) minutes.

3 When the cook time is finished, do a quick pressure release by carefully moving the sealing handle to venting and allowing all the steam to escape. When the float pin drops, unlock the lid and open it carefully.

4 Remove the cooked broccoli to a large bowl. Cover with aluminum foil and set aside.

Cheese Sauce

1 Remove the steamer basket from your pressure cooker and dump out the water. Wipe the pot dry and return to the housing unit. Press Sauté and add the butter. When the butter is melted, whisk in the rice flour, whisk continuously so the resulting roux doesn't stick to the bottom or begin to brown. Cook for 1 minute. Slowly whisk in the milk and let simmer until it just begins to thicken, stirring continuously. Add the garlic and onion powders. Add the cheese, ½ cup (60 g) at a time, so it melts completely. Adjust the seasonings if necessary.

2 Serve the cheese sauce over the steamed broccoli.

Quick and Easy Potato Salad

GLUTEN FREE • SOY FREE, NUT FREE

It's not summer without a potato salad. This quick and easy version cooks both the potatoes and hard boils the eggs at the same time. Nestle the eggs in with the potatoes and let your pressure cooker work its magic. You'll be amazed how simple it is to put together a classic summer side dish without heating up the kitchen!

Yield 6 servings

4 medium russet potatoes (or red potatoes), peeled and cubed (approximately 3½ cups, or 385 g)

3 eggs

¾ cup (180 g) mayonnaise

1 teaspoon paprika

1 teaspoon onion salt

1 teaspoon garlic powder

¼ teaspoon cracked black pepper

1 tablespoon (11 g) spicy mustard

3 tablespoons (45 g) sweet pickle relish

2 stalks celery, diced

Salt and pepper, to taste

1 Add 1 cup (235 ml) water to your inner cooking pot. Place a steamer basket over the water.

2 Place the potatoes and whole eggs in the steamer basket, nestling the eggs in with the potatoes.

3 Close and lock the lid, making sure the steam release handle is in the sealing position. Cook on high pressure for 5 minutes. When the cook time is finished, do a quick release by carefully moving the sealing handle to venting and allowing all the steam to escape. When the float pin drops, unlock the lid and open it carefully.

4 Remove the eggs to a bowl of ice water and let cool for 6 minutes.

5 Remove the potatoes to a large bowl to cool slightly. Once the potatoes are cool, add the mayonnaise, spices, mustard, relish, and celery to the bowl. Stir to combine.

6 Peel the shells from the eggs. Chop the eggs and add them to the potato mixture. Taste and adjust the seasonings. Add additional mayonnaise if desired.

7 Chill for 1 hour before serving.

BBQ Baked Beans

GLUTEN FREE • SOY FREE • NUT FREE • DAIRY FREE • EGG FREE • VEGETARIAN OPTION

Serve these sweet 'n smoky baked beans as a side dish at your next barbecue, picnic, potluck, or family dinner. It's the perfect accompaniment to our BBQ Baby Back Ribs (page 152). There is always hot debate over whether or not to soak your beans. With an electric pressure cooker, there is no need to soak beans, but for this recipe, we prefer to soak them overnight. If you choose not to soak your beans, increase the cooking time from 60 minutes to 75 minutes.

Yield 6 servings

To make your beans vegetarian, simply leave out the bacon!

1 pound (454 g) dried navy beans (optional soaking for 8 to 12 hours)

6 strips thick-cut bacon, roughly diced (Applewood Farms is gluten free)

1 medium onion, roughly diced

3 cups (705 ml) water, divided

⅓ cup (105 g) molasses

¼ cup (60 ml) maple syrup

½ cup (120 ml) tomato sauce

⅓ cup (75 g) brown sugar

1 teaspoon liquid smoke (Wright's brand is gluten free)

2 teaspoons (6 g) dry mustard powder

1 teaspoon apple cider vinegar

¼ teaspoon salt

Ground black pepper, to taste

1 Rinse and sort the navy beans, removing any stones or debris. If desired, add the beans to a bowl and cover with water to 2 inches (5 cm) above the beans. Soak for 8 hours or overnight. Drain the beans and rinse.

2 Press Sauté on your pressure cooker. When the inner pot is hot, add the bacon and cook until it begins to render. Don't let the bacon get too crisp. Add the onions to the pot with the bacon and continue to sauté until they begin to soften, 2 minutes. Add ¼ cup (60 ml) of the water to the pot and scrape up any brown bits from the bottom. Continue cooking until all the water has evaporated.

3 Add the drained beans and all the remaining ingredients to the pot. Stir well to combine.

4 Close and lock the lid, making sure the steam release handle is in the sealing position. Cook on high pressure for 60 minutes. When the cook time is finished, allow a 25-minute natural release, then do a quick release to vent any remaining steam. When the float pin drops, unlock the lid and open it carefully.

5 Discard any floating beans. Stir well. Taste a few beans for tenderness. If the beans are still hard, return the lid and cook on high pressure for another 15 minutes, with a 15-minute natural pressure release.

6 Once the beans are tender, taste again for sweetness and adjust the seasonings if desired. Add more molasses or brown sugar for sweetness or more vinegar or liquid smoke for tang.

7 After cooking, if you find your beans are too watery, press Sauté and simmer until they reach your desired consistency.

Corn on the Cob with Herbed Butter

GLUTEN FREE • SOY FREE • NUT FREE • EGG FREE • VEGETARIAN

Corn on the cob is a classic summer side dish. It pairs perfectly with any kind of barbecue, and steaming them in your pressure cooker means you don't have to heat up the kitchen with a big pot of boiling water. The herbs and butter are melted at the end and everything gets tossed together in one pot. Now that's bringing this classic dish up a notch.

Yield 6 servings

6 cobs fresh corn, husked, cobs cut in half

¼ cup (56 g) unsalted butter

3 cloves garlic, minced

1½ teaspoons fresh thyme

1 teaspoon oregano leaves

2 teaspoons (2 g) finely chopped fresh parsley

½ teaspoon red pepper flakes

¼ cup (25 g) grated Parmesan cheese

1 Add 1 cup (235 ml) water to the bottom of your inner cooking pot. Place a trivet or steamer basket above the water. Place the cut cobs on the trivet in the bottom of your pressure cooker. Stand the cobs upright so they will fit.

2 Close and lock the lid, making sure the steam release handle is in the sealing position. Cook on high pressure for 3 minutes. When the cook time is finished, allow 4 minutes of natural pressure release, then turn the handle to venting, releasing any remaining steam. When the float pin drops, unlock the lid and open it carefully.

3 Using tongs, carefully remove the corn cobs to a serving plate. Use the same tongs to remove the trivet or steamer basket. Use pot holders to lift out the inner pot and pour out any remaining water. Wipe out the pot with a paper towel, dry it, and place it back in the pressure cooker.

4 Press Sauté. When the pot is hot, add the butter to melt. Once the butter is melted, add the garlic, thyme, oregano, parsley, and red pepper flakes. Stir constantly just long enough to allow the garlic to become fragrant, about 30 seconds. Gently brush the melted butter mixture over the corn cobs. Sprinkle the Parmesan cheese over the top. Serve immediately.

Sweet and Easy Corn Bread

GLUTEN FREE • SOY FREE • NUT FREE

This is one of those recipes that doesn't require a lot of time or effort. Its simplicity will have you coming back to it again and again. The honey offers sweetness to counter the tang of the buttermilk. It is perfect for smearing with butter and honey and enjoying with some hot tea for an afternoon snack! The addition of fresh corn brings an extra layer of flavor to this bread. Make it in the morning, so it's ready to go for dinner.

Yield 6 servings

⅓ cup (47 g) Bob's Red Mill medium-grind gluten-free yellow cornmeal

1 cup (120 g) Bob's Red Mill Gluten-Free 1-to-1 Baking Mix

1 tablespoon (8 g) baking powder

1 teaspoon salt

¼ cup (56 g) unsalted butter, melted

¼ cup (80 g) honey

½ cup (120 ml) buttermilk

1 large egg

¾ cup (113 g) sweet yellow corn, fresh, frozen, or canned

1 cup (235 ml) water for the bottom of the pot

1 Spray a 7 x 3-inch (18 x 7.6 cm) cake pan with nonstick cooking spray. Set aside.

2 In a large bowl, combine all the ingredients until just mixed. Don't overmix the batter. Pour the batter into the prepared pan. Allow the batter to sit for at least 15 minutes before baking. When you're ready to bake, spray a piece of aluminum foil with nonstick cooking spray and cover the pan tightly (spray side down), crimping the edges to seal.

3 Pour 1 cup (235 ml) water into the inner pot of your pressure cooker. Place a trivet in the pot over the water. Use a foil sling (see page 18) and gently lower the filled pan onto the trivet.

4 Close and lock the lid, making sure the steam release handle is in the sealing position. Cook on high pressure for 25 minutes. When the cook time is finished, do a quick pressure release by carefully moving the sealing handle to venting and allowing all the steam to escape. When the float pin drops, unlock the lid and open it carefully. Remove the pan from the inner pot. Remove the foil cover and allow the corn bread to cool for 10 minutes before slicing into wedges and serving.

This corn bread is best eaten the day you make it, but will keep for several days, well wrapped in the refrigerator.

Spanish Rice

GLUTEN FREE • SOY FREE • NUT FREE •
EGG FREE • VEGETARIAN OPTION

This Spanish rice is delightful served with tacos or enchiladas, but it also pairs well with a juicy steak! In this recipe, we sauté the rice first in order to give it a toasted, almost nutty flavor. This little step brings a lot of extra flavor to the dish.

Yield 6 servings

2 tablespoons (28 g) unsalted butter

2 cups (380 g) long-grain white rice

1 medium onion, diced

2 teaspoons (6 g) minced garlic

1¾ cups (411 ml) chicken stock (page 213)

1 cup (235 ml) tomato sauce

1 tablespoon (8 g) ground cumin

2 teaspoons (6 g) chili powder

1 teaspoon dried oregano

¼ cup (4 g) chopped fresh cilantro

Zest and juice of 1 lime

1 Press Sauté on your electric pressure cooker. When the inner pot is hot, add the butter and dry rice. Sauté for 2 minutes.

2 Stir in the onion and continue to sauté until the onion is translucent, another 2 minutes. Add the garlic and cook an additional 30 seconds, until fragrant. Press Cancel.

3 Add the chicken stock, tomato sauce, cumin, chili powder, and oregano in with the rice.

4 Close and lock the lid, making sure the steam release handle is in the sealing position. Cook on high pressure for 12 minutes. When the cook time is finished, allow a 5-minute natural release, then do a quick release to vent any remaining steam. When the float pin drops, unlock the lid and open it carefully.

5 Transfer to a serving bowl, add the cilantro, lime juice, and lime zest. Fluff the rice with a fork and serve!

Note: To make this rice vegetarian, replace the chicken stock with vegetable stock for an equally delicious option.

Mashed Potatoes

GLUTEN FREE • VEGETARIAN • SOY FREE • NUT FREE

Mashed potatoes are the most versatile of side dishes. One of the best things about this recipe is you don't need to drain the potatoes after you cook them. Simply use an immersion blender to create smooth, fluffy mashed potatoes. To make garlic mashed potatoes, simply add several cloves of fresh, peeled, minced garlic to the potatoes and cook as directed! Serve with our Roast Turkey Breast and Easy Gravy (page 126), Southwestern Meatloaf (page 137), or your own favorite dishes. Our families love the flavor of red potatoes for mashed potatoes, but feel free to use any type of potato in this recipe.

Yield 4 servings

2 pounds (808 g) medium red potatoes, peeled and quartered

1 cup (235 ml) water

½ to ¾ cup (120 to 180 ml) milk

¼ cup (56 g) unsalted butter

¼ teaspoon salt

¼ teaspoon cracked black pepper

1 Add the potatoes and water to the inner pot of your electric pressure cooker.

2 Close and lock the lid, making sure the steam release knob is in the sealing position. Cook on high pressure for 10 minutes. When the cook time is finished, do a quick pressure release by safely moving the sealing knob to the venting position and allowing the steam to escape. When the float pin drops, unlock the lid and open it carefully.

3 Add the milk, butter, salt, and pepper to the potatoes. No need to take out the potatoes to drain them; you can mash them in the pot. Use an immersion blender or potato masher and mash until the desired consistency is reached. Taste and adjust the seasonings as needed.

4 Serve with your favorite gluten-free gravy or an extra pat of butter!

You can easily double this recipe without adding extra cook time. Even though the time doesn't double, you'll need to double the seasonings so the flavor doesn't get diluted.

Cheesy Au Gratin Potatoes

GLUTEN FREE • NUT FREE • SOY FREE • VEGETARIAN

Always at home on any dinner table, these versatile cheesy potatoes are the perfect side dish for any number of entrées. The combination of two different cheeses and sour cream to create a silky cheese sauce, along with a crunchy topping of gluten-free panko bread crumbs, creates a delectable side dish everyone will love. Watch the potatoes carefully in the broiler so the topping doesn't get too brown. Use these cheesy potatoes as an accompaniment to our Roast Turkey Breast with Easy Gravy (page 126), Classic Whole Baked Chicken (page 128), or BBQ Baby Back Ribs (page 152).

Yield 6 servings

Switch things up by experimenting with different cheese combinations for the sauce. Sharp cheddar, Parmesan, Swiss, or pepper Jack would all be delicious in this recipe. Keep the portions the same and you'll have an endless variety of potato dishes to go with any meal!

2 tablespoons (28 g) unsalted butter

1 medium onion, chopped

2 cloves garlic, minced

1 cup (235 ml) vegetable stock (page 214)

½ teaspoon salt

¼ teaspoon freshly cracked black pepper

6 medium russet potatoes, peeled and sliced ⅛ inch (3 mm) thick

1 cup (55 g) gluten-free panko bread crumbs

3 tablespoons (45 ml) melted unsalted butter

½ cup (120 g) sour cream

½ cup (60 g) shredded mild cheddar cheese

½ cup (60 g) shredded Gruyère cheese

1 Press Sauté or Browning on your electric pressure cooker. When the inner pot is hot, add the 2 tablespoons (28 g) butter. When the butter is melted, add the onion and cook, stirring occasionally, until tender, about 5 minutes. Add the garlic and cook for an additional 30 seconds, until fragrant. Add the stock, salt, and pepper, scraping up any browned bits from the bottom of the pot.

2 Add a steamer basket to the bottom of your pot over the onion and garlic mixture. Place the sliced potatoes in the basket. Close and lock the lid, making sure the steam release valve is in the sealing position. Cook on high pressure for 7 minutes.

3 Meanwhile, preheat your broiler and grease a 9 x 13-inch (23 x 33 cm) casserole dish. In a small bowl, combine the panko bread crumbs with the 3 tablespoons (45 ml) melted butter. Set aside.

4 When the potatoes are finished cooking, use the quick release method by opening the release handle and venting all the steam. When the float pin drops, unlock the lid and open it carefully.

5 Remove the potatoes and the steamer basket. Place the potatoes into the prepared casserole dish. While the pot is still hot, add the sour cream and both of the cheeses to the cooking liquid in the pressure cooker. Stir until the cheese is melted and smooth.

6 Carefully pour the cheese sauce over the cooked potatoes and stir gently to combine. Top the potatoes with the bread crumbs. Place under the broiler for 5 to 6 minutes, or until the topping is golden brown.

"Hits the Spot" Brussels Sprouts

GLUTEN FREE • VEGETARIAN OPTION •
SOY FREE • EGG FREE

These family-favorite Brussels sprouts really hit the spot when the weather cools down and fall is in the air. The salty-sweet combination of bacon paired with the bright green sprouts and the tart apples and cranberries is the quintessential holiday dish. We can't get enough of the creamy cheese and crunchy hazelnuts on top either! It's flavorful comfort food that pairs perfectly with pork and turkey dishes.

Yield 6 servings

2 tablespoons (30 ml) olive or vegetable oil

6 strips of gluten-free bacon, chopped (optional)

⅓ cup (79 ml) apple cider vinegar (Braggs brand is gluten free)

¼ cup (60 ml) maple syrup

1 teaspoon ground ginger

1 teaspoon salt

1 teaspoon coarsely ground pepper

2 pounds (907 g) fresh Brussels sprouts, trimmed and cut in half

2 large Fuji apples, peeled, cored, and diced

¼ cup (30 g) dried cranberries

½ cup (58 g) chopped hazelnuts, toasted

¼ cup (38 g) crumbled goat cheese

1 Press Sauté on your electric pressure cooker. When the inner pot is hot, add the oil. Add the chopped bacon and cook until crisp and crumbly. Move the bacon to a paper towel-lined plate, but leave the drippings in the pan. Set the bacon aside. Press Cancel.

2 Add the cider vinegar, maple syrup, ginger, salt, and pepper to the pot and whisk to combine with bacon drippings. Add the Brussels sprouts, apples, and dried cranberries, tossing well to coat.

3 Close and lock the lid, making sure the steam release knob is closed in the sealing position. Cook on high pressure for 1 minute. When it is finished, use a quick release by opening the release knob and venting the steam. When the float pin drops, unlock the lid and open it carefully.

4 Serve the Brussels sprouts sprinkled with the reserved bacon, hazelnuts, and crumbled goat cheese.

Green Bean Casserole with Fried Onions

GLUTEN FREE • SOY FREE • NUT FREE

Everyone's favorite holiday dish, this green bean casserole has a creamy mushroom sauce over tender green beans and is made completely from scratch, without using any canned soup, which could contain hidden gluten. The fried onion topping uses tapioca flour to create a thin, crispy breading that adds to the classic flavor of this dish. It is decadent enough to satisfy everyone at your dinner table, whether they eat gluten or not.

Yield 6 servings

For the green beans

2 tablespoons (28 g) unsalted butter

1 large onion, halved and thinly sliced

5 cloves garlic, finely diced

1 pound (454 g) button mushrooms, sliced

1 teaspoon salt

1½ pounds (680 g) fresh green beans

¼ teaspoon ground nutmeg

½ teaspoon red pepper flakes

1 cup (235 ml) vegetable stock (page 214)

3 tablespoons (34 g) diced roasted red bell peppers

½ cup (120 ml) heavy cream

2 tablespoons (30 ml) cold water (optional)

2 tablespoons (16 g) cornstarch (optional)

For the fried onion topping

Vegetable oil, for frying

3 tablespoons (24 g) tapioca flour

1 teaspoon salt

¼ teaspoon black pepper

1 medium onion, thinly sliced into rings

Green Beans

1 Press Sauté on your electric pressure cooker. When the inner pot is hot, add the butter. When the butter has melted, add the onion and cook for 5 minutes, or until softened and just beginning to brown. Add the garlic and cook for an additional 30 seconds, until fragrant.

2 Add the sliced mushrooms to the onions, sprinkle with the salt, and cook for 3 minutes, stirring occasionally. Press Cancel while you prepare the green beans.

3 Rinse the green beans under cold water and trim the ends. If the green beans are too long, cut them in half so they will fit into your pressure cooker. Add the green beans, nutmeg, red pepper flakes, and vegetable stock to the mushrooms and onions in the pot. Stir to combine.

4 Close and lock the lid, making sure the steam release knob is in the sealing position. Cook on high pressure for 1 minute. When it is finished, use a quick release by opening the release knob and venting all the steam. When the float pin drops, unlock the lid and open it carefully.

5 Add the roasted red bell peppers and heavy cream to the green beans. Stir until well combined. If the mixture is too thin for your liking, make a slurry by mixing the cold water and cornstarch in a small bowl and whisking until the mixture is smooth. Add the slurry to the beans and stir until it thickens. Press Cancel, but return the lid to keep the beans warm. Spray an 8-inch (20.3 cm) casserole dish with nonstick cooking spray and set aside.

Fried Onion Topping

1 In a medium saucepan, heat 1 inch (2.5 cm) of vegetable oil to 375°F (190°C).

2 In a bowl, combine the tapioca flour, salt, and pepper. Stir gently to combine. Add the thinly sliced onions and toss with your hands until the onion is well coated with flour.

3 Very gently shake any excess flour off the onion rings and carefully place a few at a time into the hot oil. Fry the onions in small batches until golden brown and crispy. When they are done, remove the onions from the oil with a slotted spoon and drain them on a paper towel–lined plate.

4 When all the onions are done cooking, open the lid of your pressure cooker and transfer the green bean mixture to the prepared casserole dish. Spread the fried onions over the green beans and place the dish under the broiler for 3 to 4 minutes, until heated through and crispy on top.

Savory Corn Bread

GLUTEN FREE • DAIRY-FREE OPTION •
SOY FREE • NUT FREE

Do you miss having bread stuffing during the holidays? Here is a way to have a delicious gluten-free stuffing on your table! Make this savory corn bread a few days ahead so it can be transformed into stuffing or, if you wish, make it fresh as a side dish for our Rib Stickin' Chili (page 62). It will be delicious either way!

Yield 4 servings

1 cup (120 g) brown rice flour (Authentic Foods brand is gluten free and not gritty)

½ cup (60 g) sorghum flour (Bob's Red Mill brand is gluten free)

¾ cup (105 g) plus 2 tablespoons (18 g) medium-grind gluten-free cornmeal, divided

2 teaspoons (5 g) baking powder

½ teaspoon salt

½ teaspoon onion powder

½ teaspoon garlic powder

1 teaspoon psyllium husk powder or ½ teaspoon xanthan gum

1 teaspoon finely chopped fresh thyme

¼ cup (56 g) unsalted butter or dairy-free butter such as Earth Balance

1 cup (235 ml) milk or dairy-free milk

1 egg, lightly beaten

1 cup (235 ml) water

1 Spray a 7 x 3-inch (18 x 7.6 cm) cake pan with nonstick cooking spray, then dust with 2 tablespoons (18 g) of the cornmeal. Set aside.

2 In a large mixing bowl, combine the two flours, remaining ¾ cup (105 g) cornmeal, baking powder, salt, onion and garlic powders, psyllium husk powder, and thyme. Whisk together until thoroughly blended.

3 In a microwave-safe bowl, melt the butter and whisk into the flour mixture; add the milk and beaten egg. Whisk to combine all of the ingredients and stir until smooth.

4 Pour into the prepared baking pan and tap lightly on the counter to release any air bubbles. Spray a square of aluminum foil with nonstick cooking spray and place (sprayed side down) over the corn bread mixture.

5 Add the water to the inner pot of your pressure cooker. Place a trivet in the pot. Using a foil sling (see page 18), carefully lower the covered cake pan into the pot on top of the trivet.

6 Close and lock the lid, making sure the steam release knob is in the sealing position. Cook on high pressure for 35 minutes. When the cook time is finished, do a quick pressure release by carefully moving the sealing knob to venting and allowing all the steam to escape. When the float pin drops, unlock the lid and open it carefully.

7 Remove the corn bread from the pot and place on a cooling rack. Remove the foil from the top and let the corn bread cool to room temperature.

Corn Bread Stuffing

GLUTEN FREE • DAIRY-FREE OPTION • SOY FREE

Thanksgiving and other family gatherings are all about abundance, and with this recipe everyone at your table can enjoy homemade stuffing. Full of apples, cranberries, and nuts, it is the perfect accompaniment to your turkey dinner, or serve it alongside a roasted chicken (page 128) for a nice change of pace.

Yield 6 to 8 servings

Notes: This is very important for the texture of your final product. Make sure you toast the cubes thoroughly.

There will be crumbs left over from making the stuffing. Don't toss them out! Save them and use them as a crumbly corn bread topping for your salad!

2 recipes Savory Corn Bread (page 188), cooled and cut into ½-inch (13 cm) cubes

1 cup (225 g) unsalted butter or Earth Balance butter substitute, divided

2 packets (12 g each) turkey-flavored Savory Choice Liquid Stock Concentrate)

1 large onion, chopped

4 stalks celery, chopped

1 large shallot, sliced

10 large fresh sage leaves, finely chopped

Leaves from 2 sprigs fresh thyme

2 sweet apples, such as Gala or Fuji, washed, cored, and chopped

1½ cups (220 g) dried sweetened cranberries

1 cup (150 g) pecan halves, coarsely chopped

Kosher salt and freshly ground black pepper, to taste

1 egg, beaten

1½ to 2 cups (355 to 470 ml) turkey or chicken stock (page 213)

1 Preheat the oven to 400°F (200°C, or gas mark 6).

2 Spread the cubes on a baking sheet. Melt ¼ cup (56 g) of the butter and mix it with the turkey-flavored concentrate. Drizzle on top of the corn bread ubes. Toss gently and place in the oven. Bake the cubes for 30 minutes, stirring every 8 to 10 minutes, until they are toasted and completely dried out. Remove from the oven and let cool to room temperature.

3 Turn the oven down to 350°F (180°C, or gas mark 4). Lightly butter a 9 x 13-inch (23 x 33 cm) baking pan; set aside.

4 In a large skillet, melt ¼ cup (56 g) of the butter over medium heat. Sauté the onion and celery for about 4 minutes and then add the shallot and sage. Continue cooking until the vegetables are softened and starting to brown, an additional 3 to 4 minutes. Remove from the heat and transfer to a large mixing bowl to cool.

5 Add the cooled corn bread cubes to the vegetables. Just use the cubes and leave behind the crumbs. (See Note, left.)

6 Add the thyme, apples, cranberries, and pecans to the corn bread mixture. Toss until evenly distributed. Melt the remaining ½ cup (112 g) butter in the microwave, then add it to the bowl and toss again. Taste and adjust the seasonings. Stir in the beaten egg and turkey stock and transfer to the prepared baking pan.

7 Bake for about 45 minutes, or until the bread is golden brown and crusty on top.

9

DELIGHTFUL DESSERTS

Eating gluten free doesn't mean you can't indulge your sweet tooth with delightful and decadent desserts. We make no apologies about loving dessert. Anything and everything chocolate for us, please! While using an electric pressure cooker for "baking" isn't immediately obvious, it is one of the best features.

When you cover a baking dish, the heat in the pressure cooker creates an oven-like setting. Using steam creates a moister environment, which is especially well suited for cheesecakes. If you've ever fought with a leaking springform pan in a pan of water, you will love the results you get in today's pressure cookers!

The key to successful gluten-free baking is a gluten-free flour blend. We've included a recipe to make your own blend (less expensive if you bake often), or you can use a store-bought variety. A few of our favorites are Bob's Red Mill 1-to-1, Cup4Cup, and Pamela's All-Purpose Gluten-Free Flour, all readily available in grocery stores and online.

Enjoy our Double Chocolate Fudge Cheesecake (page 204), Apple Cinnamon Raisin Bread Pudding (page 192), and more—all made gluten free. For the times you don't want to share, you can make Individual Key Lime Cheesecakes (page 202) or Easy Individual Mini

Cakes (page 199). Just be sure to hide the evidence. If baking isn't your thing, try the Marvelous Mocha Pudding with Homemade Whipped Cream (page 201) or the Coconut Mango Sticky Rice (page 200). They're all delicious!

Our collection of dessert recipes will have you and your family racing back to the table for seconds. You may have to live gluten free, but that doesn't mean having to sacrifice flavor or special desserts.

Recipes

Apple Cinnamon Raisin Bread Pudding

GLUTEN FREE • SOY FREE • VEGETARIAN

Bread pudding is an all-time favorite dessert. This homemade version is packed with fruit and has a sweet, fluffy custard and a sinfully delicious vanilla sauce that is caramel-like in consistency. We call it perfection on a plate and because it's made with gluten-free cinnamon raisin bread, we can enjoy it anytime!

Yield 6 servings

For the bread pudding

2 tablespoons (28 g) unsalted butter, melted, plus more for the pan

½ cup (100 g) dark brown sugar

2½ cups (590 ml) whole milk

4 eggs, beaten

2 teaspoons (10 ml) gluten-free vanilla extract

1 teaspoon ground cinnamon

½ teaspoon ground nutmeg

¼ teaspoon salt

8 cups (400 g) cubed gluten-free cinnamon raisin bread (such as Udi's brand)

½ cup (75 g) chopped pecans, toasted

2 medium baking apples (Honeycrisp or Braeburn work beautifully), peeled, cored, and chopped into a medium dice

1½ cups (355 ml) water

For the sweet vanilla sauce

½ cup (112 g) unsalted butter

½ cup (100 g) granulated sugar

½ cup (100 g) dark brown sugar

¼ teaspoon salt

1 tablespoon (15 ml) gluten-free vanilla extract

½ cup (120 ml) heavy whipping cream

(continued)

If you can't find gluten-free cinnamon raisin bread, you can substitute any other hearty gluten-free bread and add ½ cup (75 g) raisins and an extra 3 tablespoons (36 g) sugar to the recipe.

Bread Pudding

1 In a large bowl, whisk together the 2 tablespoons (28 g) butter, brown sugar, milk, eggs, vanilla, spices, and salt. Add the cubed bread, toasted nuts, and apple pieces. Mix until well combined. Set aside while you prepare the pan.

2 Using either a 6-cup (1410 ml) Bundt or 1½-quart (1.4 L) round baking dish, butter the bottom and sides of the pan. Be sure to get into the corners of the pan. Pour the bread pudding mixture into the prepared pan.

3 Place a trivet in your pressure cooker. Add the water to the bottom of the pot. Spray a piece of aluminum foil with nonstick cooking spray and place (sprayed side down) over the bread pudding. This will protect the pudding from excess moisture while cooking. Use a foil sling (see page 18) to lower the bread pudding onto the trivet.

4 Close and lock the lid, making sure the steam release knob is in the sealing position. Cook on high pressure for 25 minutes. When the cook time is finished, use the quick release method by turning the release knob to the venting position and releasing the steam. Once the float pin drops, unlock the lid and open it carefully.

5 Use the foil sling to remove the dish from the pressure cooker. If you like a crispy top, place your dish on a sheet pan and put in the oven at 400°F (200°C, or gas mark 6) for 5 minutes. Watch the bread pudding carefully so it doesn't get too brown.

Sweet Vanilla Sauce

1 While the bread pudding is in the oven, or during the last 10 minutes of cooking time, make the sweet vanilla sauce. In a small pan, combine all the sauce ingredients. Place over medium heat, stirring constantly, until the butter has fully melted and the sauce thickens, 5 to 8 minutes.

2 Cut the bread pudding into pieces, then pour some sauce over each piece. Serve warm and try not to lick the spoon!

Rice Pudding with Raisins

GLUTEN FREE • NUT FREE • SOY FREE • VEGETARIAN

This rice pudding is sweet, thick, and so creamy. We've used raisins, but feel free to make this recipe your own by adding different dried fruits or nuts. It would be great with dried mango or cranberries. The raisins don't have to be soaked in boiling water—you can soak them in orange juice or even apple juice for a sweeter flavor. If you can't find Arborio rice, use any short-grain (not instant) white rice.

Yield 6 servings

1 cup (150 g) raisins
1 cup (235 ml) boiling water
1½ cups (270 g) Arborio rice
¾ cup (144 g) sugar
½ teaspoon salt

5 cups (1175 ml) milk
2 eggs
1 cup (235 ml) half-and-half
2 teaspoons (10 ml) gluten-free vanilla extract

1 In a medium bowl, combine the raisins and boiling water. Cover and set aside for 30 minutes to plump the raisins. Note: If using juice or other liquid to plump the raisins, you do not need to boil the liquid. Just cover and soak for at least 30 minutes or up to 2 days in the refrigerator.

2 Combine the rice, sugar, salt, and milk in the inner pot of your electric pressure cooker. Press Sauté or Browning and bring to a boil, stirring constantly to dissolve the sugar. As soon as the mixture comes to a boil, press Cancel, then close and lock the lid, making sure the steam release knob is in the sealing position.

3 Cook on low pressure for 15 minutes. When the rice is finished, allow a 10-minute natural pressure release. After 10 minutes, turn the knob to the venting position, releasing any remaining steam. When the float pin drops, unlock the lid and open it carefully. Press Cancel.

4 While the rice is cooling, whisk together the eggs, half-and-half, and vanilla in a medium bowl. Carefully pour the mixture into the pot with the rice. Stir to combine. Turn the pressure cooker back on, selecting Sauté or Browning. Stir until the rice just begins to boil.

5 When the rice is hot, drain the raisins from their soaking liquid and stir into the pot. Serve immediately or pour into a large serving dish to chill. The pudding will thicken as it cools, so you may want to add a little extra half-and-half if you plan on serving it cold.

New York–Style Cheesecake

GLUTEN FREE • SOY FREE

This is a lovely adaptation of a classic New York–style cheesecake. Using ground almond meal and brown sugar in place of graham crackers will remind you of the flavors of a traditional graham cracker crust without the gluten. The pressure cooker mimics the process of baking cheesecake in a water bath, and the moisture inside the pressure cooker helps reduce the possibility of your cheesecake developing cracks. For the smoothest possible cheesecake, make sure all your ingredients are at room temperature before you begin.

Yield One 7-inch (18 cm) cheesecake

Use a 7 x 3-inch (18 x 7.6 cm) springform or push pan for this recipe. It fits perfectly in the inner pot of a 6-quart (5.4 L) pressure cooker and can be used for a variety of sweet or savory recipes!

For the crust

2 cups (224 g) almond meal (Bob's Red Mill brand is certified gluten free)

¼ teaspoon salt

1½ tablespoons (18 g) brown sugar

¼ cup (56 g) unsalted butter, melted

For the cheesecake

1 pound (454 g) cream cheese, at room temperature

2 tablespoons (16 g) cornstarch

⅔ cup (128 g) granulated sugar

Pinch of salt

½ cup (120 g) sour cream, at room temperature

2 teaspoons (10 ml) gluten-free vanilla extract

⅛ teaspoon gluten-free almond extract

2 large eggs, at room temperature

1 cup (235 ml) cold water for the bottom of the pot

Crust

1 Prepare a 7 x 3-inch (18 x 7.6 cm) springform pan by lightly spraying the bottom and sides with nonstick cooking spray (the kind without flour in it).

2 Cut a circle of parchment paper the same size as the bottom of your springform pan. Place the parchment circle on the bottom of your pan and spray with additional nonstick spray. Go lightly on the spray; you don't need a lot. Set aside.

3 In a small bowl, mix together the almond meal, salt, and brown sugar. Add the melted butter and stir with a fork until the mixture sticks together.

4 Pour the crust mixture into the prepared pan. Spread with your fingers and press down gently to form an even layer. Place the pan in the freezer while you make the cheesecake batter.

Cheesecake

1 In a medium mixing bowl, beat the cream cheese with a hand mixer on low speed, until smooth. In a small mixing bowl, combine the cornstarch, granulated sugar, and salt. Add half the sugar mixture to the cream cheese and beat until just incorporated. Scrape down the sides of your bowl with a spatula. Add the remaining sugar mixture and beat until just incorporated. Add the sour cream and vanilla and almond extracts to the cream cheese mixture. Beat until it just comes together.

2 Add the eggs, one at a time, scraping down the bowl well after each addition. Do not overmix.

3 Remove the crust from the freezer and tightly wrap the bottom of the pan with aluminum foil. This will help prevent leaks. Pour the cream cheese batter over the well-chilled crust. Tap lightly on the countertop to remove any big air bubbles. Cover the top of the pan with another piece of aluminum foil. Crimp tightly to seal the edges.

4 Pour the cold water into the inner pot of your pressure cooker. Place a trivet in the pot. Use a foil sling (see page 18) to carefully place the cheesecake pan on top of the trivet. Make sure the pan is not touching the water.

5 Close and lock the lid, making sure the steam release knob is in the sealing position. Cook on high pressure for 40 minutes. When the cook time is finished, use the quick release method by turning the release knob to the venting position and releasing the steam. Once the float pin drops, unlock the lid and open it carefully. Absorb any condensation on the surface of the cheesecake by gently blotting with a paper towel.

6 Carefully remove the cheesecake and place it on a wire rack to cool to room temperature.

7 Once the cheesecake is completely cooled, place in the refrigerator for at least 6 to 8 hours, preferably overnight. When ready to serve, remove the cheesecake from the refrigerator. Release the sides of the springform pan and run a thin knife between the parchment paper and the crust to remove, and then slide carefully onto a serving plate.

Spiced Peaches

GLUTEN FREE • SOY FREE • DAIRY FREE • VEGETARIAN • NUT-FREE OPTION

These spiced sliced peaches are a delicious gluten-free treat and are so simple to make. Just three steps and you'll have a delightful dessert ready to go in no time. They're perfect paired with our homemade yogurt (page 30), spooned over ice cream or pound cake, or with your morning oatmeal (page 32) for an extra-special breakfast treat!

Yield 4 servings

1¼ cups (295 ml) water

½ cup (112 g) packed brown sugar

1 tablespoon (8 g) ground cinnamon

½ teaspoon ground ginger

⅛ teaspoon ground nutmeg

1 teaspoon salt

6 firm peaches, peeled, pitted, and sliced into 8 pieces each

¼ cup (26 g) chopped pecans, for garnish (optional)

1 In a medium bowl, combine the water, brown sugar, spices, and salt. Press Sauce on your electric pressure cooker. Add the syrup to the pot and stir constantly until the mixture is bubbly and the sugar has dissolved. Press Cancel. Allow the syrup to cool in the pot for 20 minutes.

2 Add the peach slices to the inner pot of your pressure cooker. Stir to coat in the cooled syrup. Close and lock the lid, making sure the steam release handle is in the sealing position. Cook on high pressure for 3 minutes. When the cook time is finished, press Cancel and do a quick pressure release by carefully moving the sealing handle to venting and allowing all the steam to escape. When the float pin drops, unlock the lid and open it carefully.

3 Press Sauté and simmer for 3 to 5 minutes to thicken the syrup.

Easy Individual Mini Cakes

GLUTEN FREE • SOY FREE

There is no reason not to celebrate a great day with cake. Thanks to this recipe, you can whip up four individual mini cakes in less than an hour. These are perfect as a sweet treat for a kids' sleepover or for movie night at home. The vanilla cake is delicious on its own, but with four different ways to customize the flavors (see below), you've got plenty of options for eating cake every day of the week!

Yield 4 mini cakes

1⅓ cups (135 g) almond flour

4 eggs

¼ cup (60 ml) maple syrup

2 teaspoons (10 ml) gluten-free vanilla extract

½ teaspoon salt

1 cup (235 ml) cold water for the bottom of the pot

1 Combine all the ingredients in a bowl. Mix until just blended.

2 Spray the interior of four 8-ounce (235 ml) mason jars with nonstick cooking spray. Divide the batter evenly among the jars. Leave space at the top of each jar because the batter will rise as it cooks. Cover each filled jar with aluminum foil, crimping gently to seal.

3 Pour 1 cup (235 ml) water into the inner pot of your pressure cooker. Add a trivet to the bottom of the pot. Use tongs or a jar lifter to carefully lower the jars onto the trivet.

4 Close and lock the lid, making sure the steam release handle is in the sealing position. Cook on high pressure for 10 minutes.

5 When the cook time is finished, do a quick release by turning the release handle to venting and releasing all the steam. Once the float pin drops, unlock the lid and open it carefully.

6 Remove the jars to a cooling rack and remove the foil. Let sit for a few minutes before serving, as the jars will be hot.

Delicious Additions TO MIX UP THE FLAVORS OF YOUR CAKES, ADD THESE INGREDIENTS IN STEP 1.

DOUBLE CHOCOLATE

2 tablespoons (16 g) unsweetened cocoa powder

1 tablespoon (11 g) mini chocolate chips (Enjoy Life brand is gluten free)

RASPBERRY WHITE CHOCOLATE

½ cup (60 g) fresh raspberries or fresh strawberries, hulled and diced

1½ tablespoons (16 g) white chocolate chips (Enjoy Life brand is gluten free)

APPLE PIE

½ cup (60 g) shredded apple

½ teaspoon ground cinnamon

¼ teaspoon ground nutmeg

CARROT CAKE

½ cup (55 g) shredded carrot

1½ tablespoons (13 g) raisins

½ teaspoon ground cinnamon

Coconut Mango Sticky Rice

GLUTEN FREE • SOY FREE • NUT FREE

Any trip to a Thai restaurant when mangoes are in season must include having a dish of coconut mango sticky rice for dessert. There is something about the rich coconut flavor combined with sweet rice and juicy mangoes that is the perfect ending to a spicy meal. The fact that you can make it in your pressure cooker means you can have it for breakfast, lunch, or any other time the craving strikes. If your local store doesn't carry sweet Thai rice, you can substitute Arborio rice or any other short-grain white rice. If you do, you may need to add a touch more sugar to your dish.

Yield 6 servings

Cream of coconut is in the spirits and wine section of most grocery stores. It is used for making mixed drinks and cocktails and will add a super punch of coconut flavor to your sticky rice.

1 cup (190 g) glutinous rice or sweet Thai rice

1½ cups (355 ml) water

1 (13.5-ounce, or 378 g) can full-fat coconut milk

¼ to ⅓ cup (50 to 65 g) sugar, to taste

¼ cup (60 ml) cream of coconut

½ teaspoon salt

2 ripe mangoes

1 tablespoon (8 g) black or white toasted sesame seeds, for garnish

2 cups (470 ml) water for the bottom of the pot

1 Add 2 cups (470 ml) water to the inner pot of your pressure cooker. Put the trivet in the bottom.

2 Place the rice in a fine-mesh strainer and rinse under cold water until the water runs clear, about 1 minute. Drain the water and let sit for a minute.

3 When nearly dry, place the rice in a 1½-quart (1.4 L) casserole dish or stainless steel bowl. Add the 1½ cups (355 ml) water to cover the rice. Make sure the rice is completely submerged in the water. Place the bowl on top of the trivet.

4 Close and lock the lid, making sure the steam release handle is in the sealing position before setting the time. Press Manual and cook on high pressure for 15 minutes. When it is finished cooking, allow a 10-minute natural release and then do a quick release to vent any remaining steam. When the float pin drops, unlock the lid and open it carefully.

5 While the rice is cooking, pour the coconut milk into a saucepan and add the sugar, cream of coconut, and salt. Let it simmer gently for 3 to 5 minutes, or until the sugar is completely dissolved. Do not boil.

6 When the rice is done, remove the pan with pot holders and, while it is still hot, pour half of the coconut sauce over the top. Stir well to coat all the rice. Continue to stir until all the sauce is absorbed. Add half of the remaining sauce to the rice and continuing stirring until the rice is well coated, but mostly absorbed into the grains.

7 Slice both mangoes down either side of the pit. Take each half and score a ¾-inch (2 cm) crisscross pattern down through the flesh, stopping at the skin. Turn the skin inside out so the mango pieces then slide a knife up between the skin and mango pieces.

8 Spoon the rice into small bowls, top with cubes of mango, sprinkle with the sesame seeds, and drizzle with the remaining coconut sauce.

Marvelous Mocha Pudding with Homemade Whipped Cream

GLUTEN FREE • SOY FREE • NUT FREE • VEGETARIAN

Is it crazy to make pudding in your pressure cooker? Absolutely not! This is one of the great things about pressure cookers, because after the pudding is assembled, you can press a button and walk away. The hardest part is waiting for this rich mocha pudding to chill before you eat it. If you're worried about portion control, we've even included a way to make the pudding in individual cups.

Yield 6 servings

For the pudding

1½ cups (355 ml) heavy whipping cream

4 ounces (112 g) semisweet or dark chocolate chips, chopped

4 egg yolks

½ cup (100 g) sugar

1 tablespoon (8 g) unsweetened cocoa powder

1 teaspoon finely ground coffee or espresso powder

1 teaspoon gluten-free vanilla extract

¼ teaspoon salt

1½ cups (355 ml) water for the bottom of the pot

For the homemade whipped cream

2 cups (470 ml) very cold heavy whipping cream

2 tablespoon (25 g) sugar

½ teaspoon gluten-free vanilla extract (optional)

Pudding

1 In a saucepan over medium heat, bring the cream to a gentle simmer. Remove from the heat and add the chocolate chips. Stir until melted, smooth, and glossy. Set aside.

2 In a large bowl, whisk together egg yolks, sugar, cocoa, ground coffee, vanilla, and salt. Slowly add the slightly cooled chocolate mixture, whisking constantly until blended.

3 Strain the pudding through a fine-mesh strainer into a 1½-quart (1.4 L) round baking dish. Cover the dish tightly with foil, crimping the edges to seal.

4 Pour 1½ cups (355 ml) water into the inner cooking pot and place a trivet at the bottom. Using an aluminum sling (see page 18), lower the pudding dish onto the trivet.

5 Close and lock the lid, making sure the steam release handle is in the sealing position.

Cook on low pressure for 22 minutes. When finished, allow a 5-minute natural release, then do a quick release. When the float pin drops, unlock the lid and open it carefully.

6 Using the aluminum sling, remove the pudding dish from the pot. Carefully remove the foil from the top and allow to cool to room temperature. Cover and refrigerate for at least 3 hours or up to 2 days.

Homemade Whipped Cream

1 Place a metal mixing bowl and the whisk attachment in the freezer for at least 30 minutes.

2 Pour the very cold heavy whipping cream, sugar, and vanilla (if using) into the cold bowl. Whisk on high speed until medium to stiff peaks form, about 1 minute.

Individual Key Lime Cheesecakes

GLUTEN FREE • NUT FREE • SOY FREE

It's a lot of fun to create individual desserts in your pressure cooker. Make them to share at a party or to keep dessert to yourself for an entire week. Key limes are smaller than regular limes and have a stronger, more acidic flavor. They make the perfect summer cheesecake, as the harvest season in the United States for Key limes is relatively short. For the smoothest possible cheesecake batter, ensure all your ingredients are at room temperature before you begin.

Yield 6 individual cheesecakes

For the crust

1¼ cups (125 g) ground gluten-free shortbread cookies (such as Pamela's brand)

1½ teaspoons brown sugar

2 tablespoons (28 g) unsalted butter, melted

Pinch of salt

For the cheesecake

8 ounces (227 g) cream cheese, at room temperature

1 tablespoon (8 g) cornstarch

⅓ cup (65 g) granulated sugar

Pinch of salt

1 tablespoon (15 ml) Key lime juice

¼ cup (60 g) sour cream, at room temperature

1 teaspoon gluten-free vanilla extract

1 tablespoon (6 g) finely grated Key lime zest, plus more for garnish

1 large egg, at room temperature

1½ cups (355 ml) water for the bottom of the pot

Homemade Whipped Cream (page 201), for serving

Crust

1 Lightly spray the insides of six 4-ounce (115 g) mason jars with nonstick cooking spray.

2 In a small bowl, mix together the crushed cookies, brown sugar, butter, and salt. Divide the cookie mixture evenly among the mason jars. Gently press the cookie crust against the bottom of the glasses.

Cheesecake

1 In a medium mixing bowl, beat the cream cheese with a hand mixer on low speed, until smooth. In a small mixing bowl, combine the cornstarch, granulated sugar, and salt. Add the sugar mixture to the cream cheese and beat until just incorporated. Scrape down the sides of the bowl with a spatula.

2 Add the lime juice, sour cream, vanilla, and lime zest to the cream cheese mixture. Beat until it just comes together. Add the egg; stir until just combined. Do not overmix.

3 Divide the cheesecake batter equally among the jars. Lightly tap the jars against the counter to release any large air bubbles.

4 Add the water to the bottom of the inner pot. Place a trivet inside the pot. Place the filled jars on the trivet, being careful the sides of the jars don't touch each other or the sides of the pot. You should be able to fit five around the edges and have space for one jar in the middle. Lightly place a large piece of foil over all the jars.

5 Close and lock the lid, making sure the steam release knob is in the sealing position. Cook on high pressure for 4 minutes. When the cook time is finished, allow a natural release for 10 minutes, then move the knob to the venting position and release any remaining steam. When the float pin drops, unlock the lid and open it carefully. Press Cancel.

6 Remove the foil and absorb any condensation on the surface of the cheesecakes by gently blotting with a paper towel. Allow the cheesecakes to cool inside the pot for 30 minutes, then remove to a cooling rack and let cool until they reach room temperature. Cover the cheesecakes with plastic wrap and place in the refrigerator for at least 6 to 8 hours, preferably overnight.

7 Serve garnished with whipped cream and additional lime zest.

This recipe calls for 4-ounce (115 g) canning jars, sometimes called quilted jelly jars. If you don't have canning jars, you can use 4-ounce (115 g) glass ramekins.

Double Chocolate Fudge Cheesecake

GLUTEN FREE • NUT FREE • SOY FREE

Two different layers of chocolate make this cheesecake every chocolate lover's dream come true. Dense and rich, a small slice goes a long way! Make sure your cream cheese is at room temperature to be completely smooth. If the cream cheese is not at room temperature, you could wind up with small white flecks in your chocolate cheesecake. When ready to serve, use a very sharp knife, dipped in hot water after each cut, to create beautifully clean slices.

Yield 8 slices

For the crust

1 (6.1-ounce, or 171 g) box gluten-free chocolate cookies

1 tablespoon (12 g) granulated sugar

¼ teaspoon salt

2 tablespoons (28 g) unsalted butter, melted

For the cheesecake

1¼ cups (219 g) semisweet chocolate chips (Enjoy Life brand is gluten free)

1 pound (454 g) cream cheese, at room temperature

¾ cup (144 g) granulated sugar

3 large eggs, at room temperature

¼ cup (60 g) sour cream

2 teaspoons (10 ml) gluten-free vanilla extract

1½ cups (355 ml) water for the bottom of the pot

Confectioner's sugar, for dusting

Crust

1 Prepare a 7 x 3-inch (18 x 7.6 cm) springform pan by spraying it with nonstick cooking spray. Cut a parchment circle the same size as the bottom of the pan and place it inside your pan. Spray again on top of the parchment. Set aside.

2 Place the cookies in the bowl of a food processor and pulse until they resemble coarse sand. Pour the cookie crumbs into a medium bowl and add the 1 tablespoon (12 g) granulated sugar and salt. Stir to combine. Add the melted butter and stir until the mixture sticks together.

3 Gently press the crumbs evenly on the bottom of the prepared pan. Use your fingers or a flat-bottom glass to help press the crust in place. Put the crust in the freezer while you make the filling.

(continued)

We used Enjoy Life Double Chocolate Handcrafted Crunchy Cookies. Feel free to substitute your favorite gluten-free chocolate cookies.

Cheesecake

1 In a medium microwave-safe bowl, melt the chocolate chips on high power, stirring every 30 seconds, until smooth and completely melted. Let cool slightly while you make the rest of the filling.

2 In the bowl of a stand mixer, beat the cream cheese until smooth and creamy. Add the ¾ cup (144 g) granulated sugar to the bowl and continue to beat until smooth. Add the eggs, one at a time, beating for 1 minute and scraping down the sides of the bowl after each addition. Beat in the sour cream and vanilla until incorporated.

3 With the mixer on low speed, slowly add the cooled melted chocolate. Mix in completely. Pour the filling into the prepared crust. Tap the dish on the counter to remove air bubbles. Gently pop any bubbles that rise to the surface with a toothpick.

4 Place a trivet in the bottom of the inner pot of your pressure cooker and add the 1½ cups (355 ml) water.

5 Tightly wrap the bottom of the springform pan in aluminum foil. Lightly spray a piece of foil with nonstick cooking spray and place (sprayed side down) over the cheesecake. Using a foil sling (see page 18), lower the pot onto the trivet.

6 Close and lock the lid, making sure the steam release knob is in the sealing position. Cook on high pressure for 56 minutes. When it is finished, use a quick release by turning the release knob to the venting position, releasing all the steam. When the float pin drops, unlock the lid and open it carefully. Press Cancel.

7 Using the foil sling, carefully lift the pan out and move to a wire cooling rack. After 1 hour, remove the foil and run a thin knife around the edges of the cheesecake to loosen it from the pan.

8 Cover with plastic wrap and refrigerate for at least 8 hours or overnight, until set.

9 Cut into 8 slices and serve with a sprinkle of confectioner's sugar on top.

Sweet Spiced Applesauce

GLUTEN FREE • DAIRY FREE • SOY FREE • NUT FREE • VEGETARIAN • VEGAN

A variety of apples will give your applesauce the best possible flavor. Our favorites are Honeycrisp, Fuji, and Braeburn, as they hold up well in the pressure cooker. No need to peel your apples for this recipe. The peels add extra nutrients, color, and flavor. The peels will get soft in the pressure cooker and then practically dissolve when blended into the applesauce. Apples tend to give off a lot of water, so you'll only need to add ¼ cup (60 ml) of liquid to make this recipe work. Once you see how simple this sweet applesauce is to make, you may never buy it from the store again.

Yield 8 cups (1960 g)

3 pounds (1.4 kg) assorted apples, cored and quartered

¼ cup (60 ml) water or unsweetened apple juice

2 whole cinnamon sticks

1 tablespoon (20 g) honey or 2 tablespoons (24 g) brown sugar (optional)

1½ tablespoons (10 g) ground cinnamon

¼ teaspoon ground nutmeg

1 Place all the ingredients in the inner pot of your electric pressure cooker.

2 Close and lock the lid, making sure the steam release knob is in the sealing position. Cook on high pressure for 5 minutes. Once the cook time is finished, allow for a complete natural release. This should take about 15 minutes. When the float pin has dropped, unlock the lid and open it carefully.

3 Remove the cinnamon sticks. Using an immersion blender, puree the apples to your desired consistency. If you don't have an immersion blender, you can use a food processor or countertop blender. Just be sure to blend in batches, as the applesauce will be quite hot!

4 Let cool and serve!

We suggest avoiding Red Delicious apples; while they are fine to eat, they don't retain a lot of flavor when they are cooked and the texture tends to get grainy.

Mexican Chocolate Pound Cake

GLUTEN FREE • SOY FREE • NUT FREE

There are simply times when your craving for chocolate needs to be satisfied. This rich, moist, dense cake with a glossy chocolate glaze is perfect for satisfying those hankerings. We've replicated the flavor profile of Mexican chocolate by using semi-sweet chocolate and plenty of cinnamon. Try pairing this pound cake with a cup of coffee on a rainy afternoon. Make it extra fancy by adding whipped cream to the top!

Yield 8 servings

1½ cups (355 ml) water

1 cup (175 g) semisweet chocolate chips, divided (Enjoy Life brand is gluten free)

¼ cup (56 g) unsalted butter, softened

1 cup (192 g) sugar

2 large eggs, at room temperature

⅓ cup (80 ml) chocolate syrup

1 tablespoon (15 ml) gluten-free vanilla extract

1⅓ cups (160 g) All-Purpose Gluten-Free Flour Blend (page 27)

½ teaspoon baking soda

1 tablespoon (7 g) ground cinnamon

¼ teaspoon salt

½ cup (120 ml) buttermilk, divided

2 tablespoons (30 ml) heavy cream

1 Pour the water into the inner pot of your pressure cooker. Add a trivet to the pot. Spray a 7 x 3-inch (18 x 7.6 cm) springform pan with nonstick cooking spray. Set aside.

2 Place ⅔ cup (115 g) of the chocolate chips in a microwave-safe bowl. Microwave on high power at 30-second intervals until the chocolate is melted and smooth, stirring well each time. Set aside.

3 In the bowl of a stand mixer, beat the butter and sugar for 6 minutes, or until the mixture is light and fluffy. Add the eggs, one at a time, beating well after each addition. Add the chocolate syrup, vanilla, and melted chocolate chips and beat until well blended.

4 In a medium bowl, whisk together the flour blend, baking soda, cinnamon, and salt. With your mixer at low speed, add half the flour mixture to the chocolate batter, blending well. Add ¼ cup (60 ml) of the buttermilk, and blend. Add the remaining flour mixture and then the rest of the buttermilk, continuing to beat at low speed until the mixture is just combined.

5 Pour the batter into the prepared pan. Spray one side of a piece of aluminum foil with nonstick cooking spray and cover the cake (sprayed side down), crimping the edges to seal. Using a foil sling (see page 18), lower the cake onto the trivet in your pressure cooker.

6 Close and lock the lid, making sure the steam release knob is in the sealing position. Cook on high pressure for 55 minutes. When the cook time is finished, allow a 10-minute natural release, then turn the knob to the venting position, releasing any remaining steam. When the float pin drops, unlock the lid and open it carefully.

7 Using the foil sling, lift the cake from the pot and place on a wire cooling rack. Remove the foil from the top and allow the cake to cool for 10 minutes. Using a narrow spatula or a slim knife, gently loosen the cake from the sides of the pan and invert onto the cooling rack. Allow to cool completely.

8 After the cake is cool, make the glaze. Microwave the remaining ⅓ cup (60 g) chocolate chips in a microwave-safe bowl at high power for 2 minutes, stirring after every 30 seconds, until smooth. Add the heavy cream and microwave for an additional 15 seconds, or until just warm through. Stir until smooth and glossy. Drizzle the glaze over the cake. Allow the cake to stand for an additional 30 minutes to 1 hour for the glaze to set before serving.

Note: Use our homemade whipped cream recipe (page 201) to turn this decadent dessert into something truly spectacular. If you're feeling particularly indulgent, add 1 teaspoon of espresso powder to the dry ingredients to really bring out the richness of the chocolate in this cake!

10 BASIC STOCKS

The foundation of many recipes is a full-bodied stock. Whether chicken, beef, or vegetable, stocks provide a tremendous boost to your recipes. You can use them for soups, stews, and sauces or to add flavor and protein to grains. They are also a great way to utilize leftover bones from steaks and roasts, the carcass from your chicken or turkey dinner, and the trimmings from your vegetables.

Rather than using water, try a stock as the liquid in your cooking. You may be surprised at the depth of flavor you get, transforming your dish into something that could be served in a restaurant. Today's electric pressure cookers give you the same taste as if you had simmered the stock for hours on the stove, but in a fraction of the time. Use the Sauté feature to warm your liquids while you are prepping and adding the remaining ingredients. Preheating the liquid will cut down on the time it takes to bring the pot to pressure because it is closer to the boiling point.

If your children don't like eating vegetables, using a vegetable stock will give them a natural dose of vitamins and minerals without them knowing! Whenever you are cooking, save the extra vegetable parings and tuck them in a resealable bag in the freezer. Keep adding to the bag and, when you have enough, you can make a quick stock. Likewise, if you have extra meat or bones left over from a meat or poultry dinner, you can do the same thing. If you don't have a use for the stock right away, or have extra, freeze it for a last-minute addition that will elevate your cooking.

Recipes

Beef Stock

GLUTEN FREE • DAIRY FREE • NUT
FREE • EGG FREE

*The difference between
canned and homemade stock
is dramatic. Homemade is so
much richer and more meaty.
This beef stock can be used
to make Beef "Barley" Soup
with Sorghum (page 61)
and a number of other
recipes. Make this ahead
and freeze in smaller
amounts to have it readily
available whenever you
feel like cooking.*

Yield About 5 cups (1175 ml)

2 pounds (908 g) beef bones, cut
into smaller pieces

1 pound (454 g) beef chuck, cut
into large cubes

1 large yellow onion, quartered

3 carrots, trimmed and coarsely
chopped

2 stalks celery, trimmed and
coarsely chopped

1 sprig fresh rosemary, well rinsed

2 bay leaves

2 tablespoons (10 g) gluten-free
beef base (such as Herb-Ox
brand), dissolved in ½ cup
(120 ml) hot water

1 teaspoon whole black
peppercorns

4½ cups (1058 ml) warm water

1 Place the bones in the inner
pot of your electric pressure
cooker and add the remaining
ingredients in the order given.
Do not go over the maximum
fill line on your pot!

2 Close and lock the lid,
making sure the steam release
handle is in the sealing position.
Cook on high pressure for
2 hours. Once the machine has
come to pressure, the clock will
count down.

3 When it is finished, let the
pressure release naturally. Turn
the steam release handle to the
venting position, releasing any
remaining steam. Unlock the lid
and open it carefully.

4 Set a colander over a very
large bowl and strain the stock.
Discard the solids. Refrigerate the stock. When the fat
hardens, skim off and discard.
Refrigerate for up to 3 days or
freeze for longer storage.

*When you are making soups and stocks, the pressure cooker
will take longer to come to pressure because you have to
bring all the liquid to a boil to create the steam it needs. Be
patient; the wait will be worth it when you taste the depth of
flavor in your recipes!*

Chicken Stock

GLUTEN FREE • DAIRY FREE • SOY FREE • NUT FREE • EGG FREE

A pot of homemade stock made from bones and "spare parts" is rich in flavor and nutrients. You can use it to make soup, to add flavor and protein to cooked grains, or as the base for a rich stew. Keep smaller portions in the freezer for quick weeknight meals.

Yield About 5 cups (1175 ml)

1 chicken carcass plus wings, backs, necks, etc. (about 2 pounds, or 908 g, total weight)

5 cups (1175 ml) cool water

1 large yellow onion, quartered

3 carrots, trimmed and coarsely chopped

2 stalks celery, trimmed and coarsely chopped

4 sprigs fresh thyme

2 teaspoons (12 g) kosher or fine sea salt

1 teaspoon whole black peppercorns

1 Place the chicken carcass and parts in the inner pot of your pressure cooker. Add the water and the remaining ingredients.

2 Close and lock the lid, making sure the steam release handle is in the sealing position. Cook on high pressure for 60 minutes. When the cook time is finished, let the pressure naturally release for 12 minutes, then turn the steam release handle to the venting position, releasing any remaining steam. Unlock the lid and open it carefully.

3 Set a colander over a very large bowl or cooking pot and carefully pour the stock through. Discard the solids. Refrigerate, covered, for up to 3 days or freeze for longer storage.

This same technique can be used to make turkey stock after Thanksgiving or any time of the year. Just add sage leaves to get that classic flavor. Divide the stock into smaller portions, place in resealable bags, and freeze flat on a baking sheet. When solid, you can stack the bags in your freezer and pull out just what you need for any recipe.

Vegetable Stock

GLUTEN FREE • DAIRY FREE • VEGETARIAN • VEGAN • SOY FREE • NUT FREE • EGG FREE

For a bolder vegetable flavor, use this stock as the base for recipes such as soups, vegetable stews, and vegetarian meals. It's so satisfying that your guests will not care there isn't meat in the dish!

Yield About 6 cups (1410 ml)

1 large onion, coarsely chopped

4 carrots, trimmed and cut into chunks

5 stalks celery, coarsely chopped

2 cups (140 g) sliced mushrooms

1 tablespoon (15 g) tomato paste dissolved in ¼ cup (60 ml) water

1 clove garlic, sliced

2 bay leaves

2 sprigs fresh thyme

3 sprigs fresh parsley

1 teaspoon kosher or fine sea salt

1 teaspoon whole peppercorns

About 6 cups (1410 ml) water

1 Place all the vegetables and seasonings in the inner pot of your electric pressure cooker. Add enough water to cover the ingredients by about 1 inch (2.5 cm). Close and lock the lid, making sure the steam release handle is in the sealing position. Cook at high pressure for 18 minutes. When the cook time is finished, let the pressure naturally release for 15 minutes, then turn the steam release handle to the venting position, releasing any remaining steam. Unlock the lid and open it carefully.

2 Set a colander over a very large bowl or cooking pot and strain the stock, pressing on the solids to extract all the liquid. Discard the solids. Taste and adjust the seasonings if needed. Refrigerate for up to 3 days or freeze for longer storage

While you can use small bits of leftover vegetables to make a stock, avoid cruciferous vegetables (cabbage, cauliflower, broccoli, Brussels sprouts, bok choy, etc.) because they add bitterness to your stock, making it unusable.

ACKNOWLEDGMENTS

From Jane

Thanks to the great team at Harvard Common Press/The Quarto Group, including Dan Rosenberg, Meredith Quinn, Karen Levy, Kristine Anderson, and Anne Re for their support, partnership, and help in making this book a reality. Thank you for your belief in us and helping make this process smooth and easy. To Leslie Stoker, agent extraordinaire: Thank you for helping guide us through this project, being our advocate and ardent supporter. We are delighted to be a part of your talented group of authors. And to Sara, my friend and fabulous partner in this crazy ride we call writing a cookbook: Your expertise and skill with pressure cooking, positive attitude, and joyful spirit are remarkable. An extraordinary teammate, it was a pleasure working together to create and shape this book.

From Sara

Writing a cookbook is never the endeavor of a single person. It takes a village! I have been blessed on this journey with a group of wonderful people, without whom this book would not exist. First, to the amazing folks at Harvard Common Press/The Quarto Group: Dan Rosenberg, Meredith Quinn, Kristine Anderson, Todd Conly, Anne Re, and their respective teams, all of whom had a hand in creating this book, we are deeply thankful for your vision, time, and talents.

To Leslie Stoker at The Stoker Agency for being our agent, friend, and advocate. Thank you for everything! To Kim Peeples, mentor, friend, all-around amazing person: I am grateful for you! To Kimberly, Gigi, and Jennifer for testing and re-testing recipes and sending such detailed feedback. You ladies are amazing! And of course, to Jane, my friend and co-author. Thank you for sharing this project with me and for having the confidence to put my name beside yours on the cover!

ABOUT THE AUTHORS

Jane Bonacci is the founder and author of *The Heritage Cook* food blog and coauthor of *The Gluten-Free Bread Machine Cookbook*. She is an expert in gluten-free baking and cooking, as well as a professional food writer and recipe developer, editor, and tester. She lives with her husband in the San Francisco Bay Area.

Sara De Leeuw is a culinary instructor, professional recipe tester/developer, and a freelance writer. She is the founder of the food blog *My Imperfect Kitchen*, where she shares that while life isn't perfect, it should always be delicious! When not in the kitchen, Sara teaches private cooking classes and hosts live public cooking demos. She lives with her husband near Los Angeles, California.

INDEX